25 CLASSIC CHINESE LOVE POEMS

Translated and Interpreted

25 CLASSIC
CHINESE LOVE POEMS

Translated and Interpreted

EURYDICE CHEN & WILLIAM R. LONG

STERLING REED BOOKS

Publisher: Stirling Reed Books

ISBN 978-1-7350927-0-6

1 3 5 7 9 10 8 6 4 2

DEDICATIONS

For Joyce, to many more decades of friendship – Eurydice

To My Children, Sydney and William, whose energy, love and insight inspire me each day – William

CONTENTS

唐
Tang Dynasty
618-907 CE

清
Qing Dynasty
1644-1911 CE

INTRODUCTION

THINKING ABOUT LOVE

To love and be loved is one of the most basic longings of human life. Without love, our lives quickly turn dry and meaningless, and we become as if wandering over a vast expanse of desert sand, alone and thirsty. Finding love can be one of the most satisfying experiences in life, giving meaning, focus and joy in the midst of the challenges of living.

Yet just because we want and need love doesn't mean that getting and keeping it is easy. Challenges and disappointments abound, from the first awkward moments in meeting the other person, to negotiating the hazards of communication and growing intimacy, and to deciding whether to continue or break off love. Then, if a pair decides to wed, the joys (and problems) are just beginning! Problems of becoming "one" when there are "two" people, coupled with issues of finance, family, conflicting desires for the future and health difficulties, often add to the challenge. And then there is the loss of a spouse, often much earlier than one could have imagined in the flush of first commitment.

This multi-faceted experience is not just felt and shared with an intimate partner, but has been written about since time immemorial. Love poetry abounds in every culture. The experience of love among humans might be surprisingly similar across cultures, but each culture also has its own way of capturing it in art, music and literature.

In this book we invite you into the immense and alluring world of Chinese love poetry. Hundreds of love poems from almost every era of Chinese history still exist; we have decided to present 25 of them to you, complete with fresh translations and line-by-line analysis. Among these 25 poem are some of the most beloved poems in Chinese history; others are probably familiar to few people.

In selecting the poems, we have been especially interested in describing the full range the experience of loving. Of course, no one collection can do complete justice to that, but among the categories that are important to us are: 1) *Wooing* the other person; 2) *Missing out* on a hopeful connection; 3) *Distance and Absence* in the committed relationship; and sadly, 4) *Losing* a partner much too early. You will discover others as you open this collection.

For example, the challenge, joy, fear, embarrassment and final triumph involved in *wooing* another can be exhilarating, as well as exhausting. We explore that theme in the familiar first poem of the 诗经, or *Book of Songs,* "Crying Ospreys." The lover targets the beloved, but she seemingly eludes him. This leads to tossing and turning and nights of uncertainty. Finally, his quest is rewarded. No doubt this is the way love is "supposed" to work, but then we include another poem from the 诗经, known in English according to its number, 76, which talks about a very unconventional way that one lover approaches the beloved—climbing over the outside walls of her home to reach her. We chuckle because we recognize the energy and allure of that kind of search.

But often love connections don't happen. *Missing* a possible connection is very difficult. We illustrate that through Cui Hu's brief poem about a love that he had forever lost, though he returned to the place where he first met the young woman. One way that love "misses" is also through age-inappropriate relationships. That lament is captured in the poignant anonymous Tang Dynasty poem "I Was Not Yet Born When You Were Born."

A third theme we explore is the idea of *distance* or *absence* of lovers. This distance is sometimes required because of the husband's military service. Sometimes we are never told the reason for the distance between lovers. It is often enough just to say, "I live at the source of the river; you live at its end..." and we can then feel the sorrow of distant lovers.

Another theme that is important for us is the experience of *losing* a spouse, often much earlier than either expected. The famous Song Dynasty poet Su Shi gives us most poignant reflections of his deceased wife, whose image returned to him in a dream, even as she was buried 1000 miles away from his current government service. The Qing Dynasty's Nalan Xingde brings us into the tremendous chill felt not simply by the weather but by the loneliness of lost love.

Many other categories and poems fill this book. It is meant to invite you, and encourage you, to appreciate this wonderful and engaging literature. One you have learned love "Chinese style," you may never want to leave this poetry.

ARRANGEMENT AND SPECIAL FEATURES OF THIS BOOK

Though the following poems can be analyzed according to the aforementioned categories, we have decided to present them chronologically. Because of its relative neglect in most poetry anthologies, we have selected five poems from the *Book of Songs*, the oldest collection of poems in Chinese and one of the five Confucian Classics. We have also placed a lot of attention on Tang and Song Dynasty poets because of their centrality in shaping the contours of the Chinese poetic tradition.

Most anthologies of Chinese poetry provide just the English translation or, sometimes, the Chinese text and the English translation of the poem. In this book, in contrast, we have provided numerous other helps in order that you might enter more deeply into the appreciation of the poems. For example, we have also included the pinyin of the poems, as well as notes to the text where there are particularly difficult translation problems. In addition, the "Poem in a Nutshell" tries to give you the essence of the poem's meaning in 100 words, while a "Background" section gives either historical or literary information to appreciate the poem. Finally, an interpretive essay seeks to analyze the ideas and language of the poem so that we might see how the poem actually works. We hope that these additional features will help you appreciate these poems and encourage you to take up your study of other poems.

We mentioned above that the pinyin, or official Romanization, is provided for all the poems. We provide it so that the poems might more easily be pronounced and as an aid to finding vocabulary words, but we do so with the following caveat. The current pinyin system was only developed about 70 years ago. Though it is dependent on earlier systems of Romanization, it really is quite different from, for example, the Wade-Giles system of the late 19th century.

Pinyin is therefore only an approximate method of providing pronunciation guidance. To make matters more complex, most of the poems presented in this volume were written more than 1000 years ago; we cannot assume that all the characters in these poems would be pronounced identically to the way they are pronounced by Chinese speakers today. Therefore, even though our pinyin rendering is an attempt to aid our own pronunciation and understanding, we need to be aware that our current system may only approximate, and not precisely mimic, the characters from antiquity.

BRIEF HISTORICAL NOTE

Chinese history is divided into Dynasties, but those Dynasties are often subdivided. For example, though the lengthy Zhou Dynasty stretched from 1046-256 BCE, it is often divided into the Western (1046-771) and Eastern (771-256) Zhou. Because of a Confucian Classic so named, a portion of the latter (771-ca 476) is known as the "Spring and Autumn" Period. Yet for our purposes we will just call it Zhou Dynasty. The Song Dynasty is also divided into the Northern and Southern Song, but for our purposes we will just refer to it as the Song Dynasty. Specific dates for each poet, when they are known, are given in each essay.

Today's scholarly consensus is that the poems in the *Book of Songs,* or 诗经, come from the Western Zhou period; they were probably compiled between the 11th and 7th centuries BCE, though the origin of almost all of them is shrouded in uncertainty. Because they arose in connection with traditional occasions, such as weddings, or welcoming a person home after military service or, as this book suggests, on the occasion of love, many of them really are timeless. They are accepted today as the oldest collection of Chinese poetry.

THE ARTWORK

Each of the four sections of this book is prefaced by the depiction of a traditional Chinese plant. Together these four, the plum (梅, Zhou Dynasty), orchid (兰, Tang Dynasty), bamboo (竹, Song Dynasty), and chrysanthemum (菊, Qing Dynasty), are known as the "four gentlemen" (四君子), with 君子 being a central concept in Confucian philosophy. They have been popular in Chinese painting because of their beauty and the moral values they suggest. The plum, boldly blossoming in winter, signifies humble strength and inner beauty. The orchid wafts its gentle spring fragrance and speaks of understated elegance. The hollow stalk of the bamboo came to symbolize tolerance and open-mindedness, as well as the flexibility to bend but not break. Finally, the chrysanthemum, blooming in the cold autumn, symbolizes the ability to withstand the rigors of that season. Together they bespeak beauty and strength, apt characteristics of these poems.

SOURCES AND FURTHER READING

Though all of the poems presented in this book have been translated into English or other European languages over the years, we found three sources of special importance not only for poems in this book but also for further reading.

First: The only complete edition of the *Book of Songs* in a European language in the last generation is the 2015 German *Das altchinesische Buch der Lieder*, edited by Rainald Simon. It presents the Chinese text, pinyin and a modern German translation, with occasional clarifying notes.

Second: A very useful guide to Chinese poetry in general, historically-arranged, is Zong-qi Cai's two volumes (one volume exposition and one volume workbook) entitled *How to Read Chinese Poetry* (Columbia UP, 2008 and 2012). He not only provides guidance on how to study and translate 100 Chinese poems, but gives a useful analysis of the historical development of Chinese poetry.

Finally, a 2003 anthology of more than 75 Chinese love poems translated by Qiu Xiaolong, entitled *Treasury of Chinese Love Poems: In Chinese and English* (Hippocrene, 2003), will be of use to all who would like to dive more deeply into this genre of poetry. Qiu only provides the Chinese text and English translation, and so the reader is often unsure of how he moved from the Chinese text to his fluent and eloquent English renderings.

The actual texts used in this collection were taken from the Baidu Encyclopedia articles for each of the poems. Often when there are controverted readings, the Baidu article will discuss alternatives and tell us why the version chosen, which is presented here, was selected.

We hope you enjoy this small sample of a great feast of Chinese love poems.

Eurydice Chen
William R Long

Salem OR
April 2019

周

ZHOU DYNASTY

1046-256 BCE

诗经·国风·周南·关雎

佚名 | 周

关关¹雎鸠，在河之洲。
窈窕淑女²，君子³好逑。

参差荇菜⁴，左右流之。
窈窕淑女，寤寐求之。
5　求之不得⁵，寤寐思服。
悠哉悠哉⁶，辗转反侧。

参差荇菜，左右采之。
窈窕淑女，琴瑟⁷友之。
参差荇菜，左右芼⁸之。
10　窈窕淑女，钟鼓乐之。

shī jīng guó fēng zhōu nán guān jū

yì míng zhōu

guān guān jū jiū zài hé zhī zhōu
yǎo tiǎo shū nǔ jūn zǐ hǎo qiú

cēn cī xìng cài zuǒ yòu liú zhī
yǎo tiǎo shū nǔ wù mèi qiú zhī
qiú zhī bù dé wù mèi sī fú
yōu zāi yōu zāi zhǎn zhuǎn fǎn cè

cēn cī xìng cài zuǒ yòu cǎi zhī
yǎo tiǎo shū nǔ qín sè yǒu zhī
cēn cī xìng cài zuǒ yòu mào zhī
yǎo tiǎo shū nǔ zhōng gǔ yuè zhī

1　关关 – "Guan Guan;" onomatopoeia for the cries of ospreys

2　窈窕淑女 – the phrase describes an attractive lady who's suitable for marriage, with implications of outer beauty but also inner virtue; we chose to render it as "graceful"

3　君子 – has a range of meanings from a gentleman, a man of noble status, to a king; we chose to render it simply as "he"

4　Floating hearts – Nymphoides peltata; a water plant

5　求之不得– to not obtain that which one pursues

6　悠哉悠哉 – describes leisure and passing of time; captures a sense of constant longing

7　琴瑟 – qin and se, classical string instruments similar to the zither

8　芼 – to select

Airs of the States·Odes of Zhou & South
Crying Ospreys·Book of Songs 1
Unknown | Zhou Dynasty

The ospreys cry on the river's isle,
There's a graceful young lady whom he would like to marry.

The floating hearts, long and short, drifting along left and right.
There's a graceful young lady, and he seeks her night and day.
He seeks her but can't find her, he thinks of her night and day.
His longing grows, his yearning grows, tossing and turning in his distress.

The floating hearts, long and short, he plucks them left and right.
There's a graceful young lady, he beckons her with strings and picks.
The floating hearts, long and short, he collects them left and right.
There's a graceful young lady, he delights her with bells and drums.

The Poem in a Nutshell

This is the most famous poem in the most famous collection of Chinese poetry—and it is about love. Though originating more than 2500 years ago, the poem speaks of themes that transcend culture and time. We have a charming and gentle young woman and a noble young man. He wants her for his wife and pursues her with eagerness. But for unspecified reasons he can't achieve his goal. As a result, he sinks into sleepless longing, tossing and turning with dreams of the beloved. Yet, he doesn't give up. Just as floating hearts are gathered and arranged, so he seeks to "gather" her. And, with the celebratory and inviting sounds of the zither and harp, bells and drums, he finally achieves his end.

Background

The 诗经 (Book of Songs) consists of 305 anonymous poems collected from throughout China during the first part of the Zhou Dynasty (11th century BCE – 3rd century BCE). One can easily imagine the poems as originating in the diverse life situations of an agricultural people, though filtered through a fairly rigid editorial process to lend a certain consistency of form to the collection. The final form aids memory and mastery not just of themes, but of the hundreds of terms for plants and living creatures that fill the pages of this classic.

The Book of Songs is one of the Five Confucian Classics, and was believed by that prominent school of thought to embody the virtues of respect for elders, social harmony and life according to the Mean. Indeed, in the Analects, Confucius even comments on this poem, the first in the Book of Songs. His memorable words are that the 关雎 is 乐而不淫，哀而不伤 or "expressive of pleasure without tending to license, and grief without wallowing in excessiveness" (Analects 3.20). In a word, Confucius saw this poem, the lead poem of the collection, as perfectly expressing the Confucian understanding of love—passionate, to a point; sad, to a point, but always staying within prescribed bounds.

Analysis

This 80-character, ten-line poem may be divided into three sections. The first two lines function as a summary of the entire poem; lines 3-6 treat the frustrating and seemingly fruitless quest for love; lines 7-10 record the triumph of love after the result of diligent search. The neatly ordered structure, frequent repetition of crucial phrases, and satisfactory result after heartfelt quest all reinforce the notion that the search for love, no matter how difficult and seemingly fruitless, will be rewarded.

The first part (ll 1-2) states the problem or issue in the poem with admirable succinctness. Using nature as a guide, with the osprey singing its eternal song, we have a young woman and a young man. She is described as 窈窕淑女, words that are generally rendered as "graceful and gentle" but the real meaning of the words is in the sound—yaotiao shunv. This is the only thing said of her—she is yaotiao shunv. Charming, delicate, graceful, gentle, virtuous, beautiful—all are ways of trying to get at an untranslatable essence. And then there is the young noble man. All that is said about him is that "he seeks her for a wife." He is in pursuit; she is all the best virtues wrapped into one. How will this unfold?

The second part (ll 3-6) begins where the summary statement ended—with the young man's pursuit. But before that pursuit is described, we have nature again entering the poem. On the surface of the stream are floating hearts, all different sizes, floating here and there. There is a looseness and uncontrolled nature to their floating captured by the words 参差 (different sizes/uneven) and 流 (floating/drifting). It is as if the floating hearts represent the hearts of all people, floating aimlessly in the river. But he is after a particular floating heart. With a repeated phrase we have, "Night and day (寤寐) he seeks her." He searches but to no avail (不得). This adds to the young man's desperation and desire. He ponders the situation, pines for her, longs for her. He lies down to sleep but he can't. The priceless four characters sum up his frustration: "tossing and turning, he can't sleep a wink" (辗转反侧).

But that isn't the end of the story. The final part (ll 7-10) describes the reward for his effort. Still the floating hearts are in the water, of all sizes, but two small verbs dropped in, in lines 7 and 9, indicate that things will change. Whereas in line 3 the floating hearts just "drifted," in lines 7 and 9, they are "gathered" and "arranged" (采, 芼) or "plucked" and "collected." Just as one can harvest floating hearts, so the "floating hearts" of potential lovers can be gathered. The young man learns this, and boldly "gathers" what only "floated" previously. And then, he brings her home, so to speak. Music is the final word in lines 8 and 10. He has "gathered" her and now he brings her to the celebratory music. The zither and harp of line 8 and the bells and drums of line 10 indicate that his quest has been successful.

诗经·国风·周南·桃夭　　**shī jīng guó fēng zhōu nán táo yāo**

佚名 | 周　　*yì míng zhōu*

桃之夭夭[1]，灼灼其华[2]。　　táo zhī yāo yāo zhuó zhuó qí huá
之子于归[3]，宜其室家。　　zhī zǐ yú guī yí qí shì jiā

桃之夭夭，有蕡其实。　　táo zhī yāo yāo yǒu fén qí shí
之子于归，宜其家室。　　zhī zǐ yú guī yí qí jiā shì

桃之夭夭，其叶蓁蓁[4]。　　táo zhī yāo yāo qí yè zhēn zhēn
之子于归，宜其家人。　　zhī zǐ yú guī yí qí jiā rén

1　桃之夭夭 gave rise to a homophonic idiom, 逃之夭夭, which means to flee

2　华 – flower

3　之子于归 – 之子 means child, in this case daughter; 于归 means to be married (exclusive to females)

4　The characters describing abundance (灼、蕡、蓁) become increasingly complex over the course of the poem, signifying ever-growing abundance

Airs of the States·Odes of Zhou & South
Lush Peach·Book of Songs 6
Unknown | Zhou Dynasty

The lush peach tree, its buds ablaze.
The gentle bride brings family joy.

The lush peach tree, its fruit abundant.
The gentle bride bears family delight.

The lush peach tree, its leaves are so splendid.
The gentle bride helps her family flourish.

The Poem in a Nutshell

Of the many thorny problems faced by those who marry, one of the sharpest is establishing and maintaining harmonious relationships with the spouse's family. With confident ease, pleasant rhythm and an arresting analogy, this poem assures the listener, whether three thousand years ago or yesterday, that those relationships will work and will flourish. The flourishing love relationship is likened to a peach tree which, in successive months and seasons, sends out its buds, its fruits and its leaves. The flaming and luxuriant buds, abundant and succulent fruit, and lush and teeming leaves all presage familial success.

Background

The poem consists of six lines and 48 characters, with the first four characters of lines 1, 3, and 5 being identical, and the first four characters of lines 2, 4, and 6 being identical. There is only minimal variation in the last four characters of lines 2, 4, and 6; indeed their variation, from 室家 to 家室 to 家人 may be dictated more by a desire to maintain rhyme (hua/jia; shi/shi; zhen/ren) than to differentiate meaning. Yet close attention to the flow and language of the poem reveals that a movement of quiet but powerful integration is happening before our eyes. The woman, who is joining her husband's people, will be the instrument of fruitfulness in her new family. One way this growing integration and fruitfulness is evident comes through counting the strokes of the Chinese characters. The word for "aflame" consists of two seven-stroke characters; for "abundant" we have one 15-stroke character; for "splendid" we have two 13-stroke characters. From 14-15-26 strokes, the characters themselves speak of a "thickening" or growing fruitfulness of the family.

No one is sure of the life situation that gave birth to the poem, though some suggest it was originally advice given by an older female relative to a new bride. The poem is normally characterized as a xìng poem, that is, one in which images from nature stimulate thinking so that the truth of the poem's subject will be made more clear. In this case the image is of the peach tree which, in successive seasons, sends forth its buds, its fruits and its leaves. Its profusion and color, fruitfulness and shade, aid us in imagining the ways that the new wife's presence will give those same things to her family.

Analysis

The poem uses three stages in the annual life of a peach tree to present a hopeful picture of familial harmony and fruitfulness. Doubled characters (夭夭, 灼灼, 蓁蓁) add a level of intensity and life to the growth of the tree. It is luxuriant in its growth and ablaze with buds. The radical 火 in the character 灼 (l 1) suggests a tree ablaze—with color, with new life, with the noiseless but powerful cycle of nature. The luxuriance and brightness of the tree in the spring presages good things for a relationship. The woman leaves her home and is integrated into the new family. Bright and fruitful beginnings get us started.

Though the second stanza (ll 3-4) seems almost to repeat the thought of the first, a substitution of two characters give movement and shape to it. The tree remains luxuriant; that doesn't change. But now we have fruit (实) appear, and the fruit is abundant and plentiful (蕡). What began with flaming buds has now matured to abundant fruit. One can imagine the natural process opening before our eyes. Yet that process is unfolded not simply for the sake of the tree but for the sake of the lesson to which it points. The woman, having entered the husband's home, brings fruitfulness to it. We try to capture the double nature of that fruitfulness by the word "bear"—she brings abundance; she bears a child.

In the West, we might think of the peach tree's phases as only two: budding and fruit, with fruit being the culmination or goal of the process. Yet not so in this poem. Our third stanza (ll 5-6) takes us further into the cycle of the tree: the leaves. The countless leaves match the buds in luxuriance and the fruit in productivity. What began as a fruit-giving process has now led to a shade-giving process. But shade for a tree symbolizes an additional level of fruitfulness in the family. Shade indicates not only that a child will come, but there will be more children and, further, that what has begun as two people, with her "going to her new home" (之子于归) has led to the creation of a 家人, a family. It is here that the last two characters of the stanza perhaps provide a sense of deeper movement than in the earlier two stanzas. She has become fully integrated in the clan, a seamless addition to a great people.

This poem is one of brimming optimism. It takes us from a promise of fruit, to the realization of fruit to the provision of shade. The poem, of course, makes it appear much more seamless than life normally is but when the good wishes are first uttered to bride and groom, they are not unlike this. Seen in this light, 桃之夭夭 almost functions as a "toast" to the new couple, a wish for a relationship and fruitfulness as abundant as the peach tree. Though simple, the wish captures the longing of nearly all who marry.

诗经·国风·召南·野有死麕   **shī jīng guó fēng zhào nán yě yǒu sǐ jūn**

佚名 | 周   *yì míng zhōu*

野有死麕，白茅包之。   yě yǒu sǐ jūn bái máo bǒu zhī
有女怀春[1]，吉士诱之。   yǒu nǚ huái chūn jí shì yòu zhī

林有朴樕，野有死鹿。   lín yǒu pǔ sù yě yǒu sǐ lù
白茅纯束，有女如玉。   bái máo chún shù yǒu nǚ rú yù

舒而脱脱[2]兮！   shū ér tuì tuì xī
无感我帨[3]兮！   wú hǎn wǒ shuì xī
无使尨也吠！   wú shǐ máng yě fèi

---

1 怀春 – literally "to hold Spring in her bosom," signifies being in love

2 脱脱 – to be slow and graceful in one's movements

3 帨 – sash or apron of traditional Chinese dress, translated as skirt

Airs of the States·Odes of Zhou & South
In the Wild Lies a Dead Deer·Book of Songs 23
Unknown | Zhou Dynasty

In the wild lies a dead deer bound in grass,
There's a young lady with love in her heart, a young man is enticing her.

Among the wild shrubs of the forest is a dead deer,
It's bound in grass, and there's a young lady as beautiful as jade.

"Easy does it!
Don't touch the skirt!
Don't make the dog bark!"

The Poem in a Nutshell

Like Book of Songs 76, discussed below, this poem reflects the excitement of two lovers who are doing all they can to keep the noise of their amorous encounter to a minimum. In Poem 76, emphasis will be on making sure that family and neighbors not be privy to the unconventional advances of the man. Here the emphasis is on not disturbing the dog, whose bark would, more than any sighs or squeals, give away the hidden delights shared by the couple. Most readers understand the imagery of the first two stanzas in courtship terms: the man has killed and tightly wrapped a deer, intended as a present for his beloved. She is aglow with love; he takes the opportunity afforded by the gift and by her mood to make his advances more explicit. Excitement is in the air!

Background

Despite attempts to identify precise circumstances contributing to the creation of many poems in the 诗经, China's earliest collection of poetry, the origins of these poems remain elusive. Many scholars refer to the 诗经 poems as natural expressions of the genuine emotion or spirit of the people. This approach also informs the treatment of 诗经 love poems, such as 野有死麕. In a supposed era of simple love and genuine passion, this poem is seen by many as a straightforward attempt of a young man to woo a woman through the gift of a prized deer which he has killed and carefully wrapped. His loyalty is reflected in the first two stanzas, as is her beauty and readiness for love. The final stanza brings us into the pulsating reality of intimate connection. We feel the heat, even after nearly 3000 years. Yet, there is an alternative and more sinister reading of the poem, which is also presented below.

Analysis

First, let's present the conventional interpretation. That interpretation argues that what we have in the poem is a traditional and pure wooing of a woman through the gift of a valuable wedding present, the dead deer. By giving her this present, the man feels empowered to approach her physically. She enjoys his present and his touch, though bashfully pushing him away under the pretext of not disturbing the dog. The poem, in this reading, is a paean to pure and innocent love.

The first stanza sets the stage for the action. Three scenes make up this stanza. First, we see a dead deer carefully tied in grass, lying in the wild. Then we see a young lady with, literally, "Spring in her heart." Spring love is fresh love, love that is triggered by the luxuriant growth of nature and the desire to share in this productive fruitfulness. Finally, we see a young man who is behind this all, having killed the deer and is now enticing the woman both with the present and, no doubt, his wooing words.

The second stanza largely repeats the thoughts of the first, adding a slightly richer description of the wild where the deer is found and subtracting out the presence of the man. Meanwhile, the woman is described briefly 如玉, "like jade," as smooth and beautiful as that precious stone.

Finally, the action picks up. He approaches her and fumbles with her garment, trying to untie it. She doesn't rebuff him but only says "slow down" or "easy does it!" Yet, her words are a bit contradictory, as is often the case between young and hesitant lovers. Go slow! Don't touch! Well, be careful! That is the spirit of the last stanza. Love is in the air.

Yet, a more sinister reading presents itself. This reading begins with the realization that nature scenes laid out in the first line of a 诗经 poem often *are* the message of the entire poem. Take 诗经 6, 桃 之夭夭, where the first four characters speak of the fruitfulness and luxuriance of the peach tree. That theme will be central for the entire poem. It celebrates the fruitfulness of the marriage and family, under the image of a fruitful peach tree. If we extend this analysis to 野有死 麕, we conclude that what is really at stake in the poem is "death in the wilderness." Death, rather than some kind of love, will be the message of the poem.

But how does this play out? This sinister interpretation rests its next point on the translation of 诱 at the end of the first stanza. We rendered it above as "entice," but it can just as well be translated as "lure" or "seduce." In this reading, the second and third scenes of the first stanza would be the woman has spring love in her heart and the man, ever watchful, knows he can take advantage of that. How does he do so? He simply seduces her. Perhaps he does so through the force of his personality or words or insistent advances, but the reality under this interpretation is that, rather than demonstrating a "purity" of love, he simply wants to take advantage of her. He will use her, and then drop her like the dead deer that is lying motionless in the first stanza. Rather than a present to a future wife, the dead deer would represent the situation of the woman after the man has fully taken advantage of her. He has enjoyed his pleasure, and she is dead and bound and covered in the forest. He exploited her vulnerability and left her like the bound deer.

诗经·国风·王风·君子于役

佚名 | 周

shī jīng guó fēng wáng fēng jūn zǐ yú yì

yì míng zhōu

君子于役，不知其期。
曷至哉？
鸡栖于埘，日之夕矣，
羊牛[1]下来[2]。
5 君子于役，如之何勿思！

jūn zǐ yú yì bù zhī qí qī
hé zhì zāi
jī qī yú shí rì zhī xī yǐ
yang niú xià lái
jūn zǐ yú yì rú zhī hé wù sī

君子于役，不日不月[3]。
曷其有佸？
鸡栖于桀，日之夕矣，
羊牛下括。
10 君子于役，苟无饥渴[4]！

jūn zǐ yú yì bù rì bù yuè
hé qí yǒu huó
jī qī yú jié rì zhī xī yǐ
yáng niú xià kuò
jūn zǐ yú yì gǒu wú jī kě

1 羊牛 – sheep and cattle
2 下来 – to descend from the hill
3 不日不月 – the waiting cannot be counted in days or months
4 苟无饥渴 – I hope he at least isn't hungry or thirsty

Airs of the States·Odes of Wang
My Husband is in Service·Book of Songs 66
Unknown | Zhou Dynasty

My husband is in service for who knows how long.
When will he return?
The chicken takes its roost, the sun goes down,
The cattle come home.
My husband is in service, how can I help but yearn?

My husband is in service for who knows how long.
When will we reunite?
The chicken has its perch, the sun goes down,
The cattle come home.
My husband is in service, I just hope he's not starving.

The Poem in a Nutshell

This poem probes a subject not often discussed when couples are in the first moments of marital connection—the reality of separation. After all, you marry for love, security, enjoyment of each other and future prospects of a growing family. Yet in many societies, particularly ancient China, long absences of the husband were the norm. Rather than loading the poem with florid sentences and deeply distraught words, the (female) speaker just makes a series of comparisons with nature or the animal world. Animals know where they belong at night—home; the sun each day goes down (and returns home), but her husband remains away. We are touched by the painful reality of nature's recognition of what constitutes normal life but of human inability to do the same.

Background

Convict as well as conscript labor played an important role in early Chinese history. During the Qin and Han Empires (evidence from the Zhou is harder to gather), most of the adult population was required to perform labor for the state at least one month per year. In addition, there were extensive requirements for garrison or actual combat service. Here the poem only says that the husband/lord is "away on service," yet that could be anything from constructing a canal, to long and boring months on a border outpost, to actual fighting. What makes the separation occasioned by the service so poignant here is that its terminus is uncertain. Separation with a fixed ending date may be difficult but one can count down the days until reunion. There is little consolation for the couple that is separated with no idea about the end of the service. But that is where our poem both begins and ends.

Analysis

The poem consists of 64 characters in two stanzas. As we are now accustomed to see in many poems from the 诗经, there is repetition, slight variation in words from stanza to stanza, skillful use of nature and the animal world to get one's point across, and an underlying longing that is usually hinted at rather than fully described. Part of the challenge and allure of the 诗经 is to see the intensity in the common language and the emotion in the repetition.

The poem's two stanzas present one problem—the speaker's husband is off on service. Though the respectful word 君子 (literally, "lord" or "gentleman") rather than 丈夫 or other terms is used at the opening of each stanza, we certainly have the context of a marital relationship. Perhaps the couple knew all along that part of husband's responsibility was to be "on service" throughout their marriage. Yet, when the reality of that "service" dawns on the woman, the one left behind in the village, it hits her with a peculiar power and loneliness.

Easy to note is the simplicity of the language and flow of each stanza. He is off on service, but the time of service is indeterminate. When, in fact, will he return? Those thoughts are not only understandable but moving. Nothing can take away the pain of separation. But then, in the second half of each stanza is the most painful realization. Three examples from the world of nature or animals are presented, and the result is the same: each of them, the bird, the sun, the cattle, knows its time. That is, each knows when it is time for shining and setting, for grazing on the hills and coming home, for flying away and coming home to the roost. Nature and animals don't have the sophistication of time-measuring devices, but they seem to know instinctively when their day is over, their service done. Why, then, is it so hard for humans to learn the same lesson? As some commentators suggest, perhaps the author and her husband had birds on the property or owned cattle; the process envisioned in the poem, then, is not an unrealistic one—she can see nature returning home every day.

This crushing reality—of husband's irregular absence when nature teaches regularity—comes home to us, the reader, through the last phrase of each stanza. In the first she asks, "How can I help but yearn?" There is no messenger, divine or human, who can bring or take a note; there is only the gaping hole of separation. How can I help but yearn? The last words of the poem, however, express not just her yearning but a well-founded fear for his well-being. She has gone from concern for self and her longing to concern for her husband's welfare. "I sincerely hope he is not without food and drink" is the sense of it.

Few deep emotions are expressed. There is no discovery of traces of the missing spouse, no odors left behind that warm and break the heart. There is just the unsolved puzzle of why nature's lessons can't be learned by humans. The quiet absence of the husband while birds coo and bill outside her window is really all that needs to be said.

诗经·国风·郑风·将仲子

佚名 | 周

shī jīng guó fēng zhèng fēng qiāng zhòng zǐ

yì míng zhōu

将仲子¹兮，无逾我里，
无折我树杞。
岂敢²爱之？畏我父母。
仲可怀³也，
5 父母之言亦可畏也。

qiāng zhòng zǐ xī wú yú wǒ lǐ
wú zhē wǒ shù qǐ
qǐ gǎn ài zhī wèi wǒ fù mǔ
zhòng kě huái yě
fù mǔ zhī yán yì kě wèi yě

将仲子兮，无逾我墙，
无折我树桑。
岂敢爱之？畏我诸兄⁴。
仲可怀也，
10 诸兄之言亦可畏也。

qiāng zhòng zǐ xī wú yú wǒ qiáng
wú zhē wǒ shù sāng
qǐ gǎn ài zhī wèi wǒ zhū xiōng
zhòng kě huái yě
zhū xiōng zhī yán yì kě wèi yě

将仲子兮，无逾我园，
无折我树檀。
岂敢爱之？畏人之多言。
仲可怀也，
15 人之多言亦可畏也。

qiāng zhòng zǐ xī wú yú wǒ yuán
wú zhē wǒ shù tán
qǐ gǎn ài zhī wèi rén zhī duō yán
zhòng kě huái yě
rén zhī duō yán yì kě wèi yě

---

1 仲子 – 仲 is the title designated to the second son of a family; here we have chosen to translate it as Mr. Zhong

2 岂敢 – literally "how dare I;" our translation makes it flow more smoothly

3 怀 – literally "bosom" or "to hold"

4 诸兄 – various (elder) brothers; refers to all older male relatives of the narrator

Airs of the States·Odes of Zheng
My Dear Zhong·Book of Songs 76
Unknown | Zhou Dynasty

My dear Zhong, don't climb into my courtyard,
Don't snap the wolfberry branches.
It's not that I care so much about the tree, rather, I fear my parents.
I hold you dear,
But I really fear what my parents say.

My dear Zhong, don't climb over my wall,
Don't snap the mulberry branches.
It's not that I care so much about the tree, rather, I fear my brothers.
I hold you dear,
But I really fear what my brothers say.

My dear Zhong, don't climb into my garden,
Don't snap the sandalwood branches.
It's not that I care so much about the tree, rather, I fear the people.
I hold you dear,
But I really fear what people will say.

The Poem in a Nutshell

This endearing poem describes a woman's feelings when love is pursued outside the safe and predictable channels presented in 关雎, the first 诗经 poem. There we saw a man's desire to make a woman his wife, pursue her with abandon, toss and turn with anxiety, and finally woo her with the sensual and dramatic music of the zither and drums. But here we have a surreptitious method. The suitor climbs into her yard, crushing trees as he gets closer and closer to the inner garden, a symbol of the lush and aromatic beauty that awaits him. With his every approaching step her anxiety rises. His method, though furtive, will set off the alarm bells in parents, siblings, neighbors.

Background

This 99-character poem bears the unmistakable marks of that first collection of Chinese poems, the 诗经. Four-character lines predominate, repeated phrases appear, and then there are phrases that repeat except for one or two characters. As the poem develops, the drama increases. As in the other poems, the subject is love, but here we have love pursued in an unconventional but probably not completely unusual manner. Rather than conforming to the predictable pattern of wooing, anxiety, and then reward, here the man audaciously leaps walls, destroys trees and finally gets closer and closer to his target, the woman. The snapping of the branches may point to the snapping of convention as the man gets nearer to the woman. She, in love with him, is put in a real bind. If she affirms his method and his passion, she may damage her family and its reputation; if she rebuffs his offer, she may lose him. Unlike *Book of Songs* 1 and 6, where rewards for faithful behavior are clearly in sight, and where all the early poem tension is resolved by the end of the poem, in this poem nothing is resolved. This poem leaves the reader wondering what would have happened if there were a *fourth* stanza. Would the man have realized the object of his desire? Would conflict have ensued? But it is good that the poem ended after three stanzas, for many lovers find themselves in similar binds— of having intense loyalty both to family and to lover, and realizing that these loyalties might just be in irreconcilable conflict.

Analysis

The three stanzas follow the movement of the man as he makes his way from the outer courtyard to the inner garden of his beloved's home. He does so through climbing over whatever obstacle is in his way. As he gets closer, the woman's fears increase. He goes from outside to inside, while her biggest fear is that the word of his movement will go from insiders (parents) to outsiders (neighbors). Part of the poem's appeal is that way that these two movements complement each other.

Each stanza begins with the same address: "My dear Zhong." Some might translate it as "Please Mr. Zhong" or "My dear sir," but our translation emphasizes the intimacy of the connection. He is her beloved;

later she will say so in more explicit terms ("I hold you dear"), but here there is just a plea. We have two negatives that follow—don't climb into the courtyard and don't snap the branches. Each of the three stanzas urges the dear Zhong not to trespass in this way. No particular significance rests on the three trees or shrubs: wolfberry, mulberry, sandalwood. They are chosen because of the rhyme scheme with the object over which he clambers, and so we have: li/qi; qiang/ sang; tan/yuan. Though heartfelt, the lines are uttered in perfect rhyme sequence.

Each of the stanzas then emphasizes the reason for her urging Zhong not to trespass. In order it is because of fear of parents, brothers, neighbors. The word of Zhong's unorthodox courting method will certainly leak out. Allegations will fly against her and her family. She will probably be accused of encouraging this reckless and honor-threatening behavior, and this action will be proof of her irresponsibility and inability to affirm the family's honor over her own selfish desires.

Yet, she truly loves the man who is clambering over the walls, snapping branches and coming closer and closer to her. Most translations of the repeated phrase 仲可怀也 render it "Of course I love you" or "Zhong I dearly love," and that becomes the nub of the problem. If he were a mere interloper, she could easily call out her brothers and protest her innocence. But he isn't. He is a lover pursuing a socially-unapproved method of gaining her. Ah—perhaps the parents had barred the front door or the brothers had expressed their displeasure, thus forcing him to this unorthodox approach. Yet it also bespeaks his desire, a desire that is willing to incur personal shame and exclusion for the sake of love. What woman would be unmoved by such desire?

The poem doesn't resolve the tension that grows with each stanza. He gets closer, the fear of rumors goes wider, her anxiety increases. Lovers face all kinds of tensions in life. One of the biggest is whether and how to confine one's love to socially-approved parameters. The poem doesn't give an answer to the question, but it touches our heart as we feel the tension rise with each stanza.

越人歌

佚名 | 周

今夕何夕兮
搴舟[1]中流，
今日何日兮
得[2]与王子同舟。
5 [3]蒙羞被[4]好兮
不訾[5]诟耻。[6]
心几烦而不绝兮
得知王子。
山有木兮木有枝，
10 心悦君兮君不知。[7]

yuè rén gē

yì míng zhōu

jīn xī hé xī xī
qiān zhōu zhōng liú
jīn rì hé rì xī
dé yú wáng zǐ tóng zhōu
méng xiū pī hǎo xī
bù zǐ gòu chǐ
xīn jǐ fán ér bù jué xī
dé zhī wáng zǐ
shān yǒu mù xī mù yǒu zhī
xīn yuè jūn xī jūn bù zhī

---

1 搴舟 – to row a boat; sometimes recorded as 搴洲

2 得 – to get to; communicates idea of privilege

3 Lines 5 and 6 have been difficult to explain and translate by all scholars due to the lack of a subject and the use of similar words that each hold a field of meanings

4 被 – to be covered in; interpreted figuratively as being overwhelmed

5 訾 – to speak badly of

6 Contrast between 蒙羞 and 诟耻; both mean humiliation and shame but 蒙羞 leans toward shyness while 诟耻 leans toward disgrace

7 枝 and 知 are homophones; although line 9 literally means "The mountain has trees, the trees have branches," the wordplay makes clear the contrast between the awareness of nature in line 9 and the ignorance of man in line 10

Song of the Yue
Unknown | Zhou Dynasty

What a night! Such a night,
Rowing about mid-stream.
What a day! Such a day,
Sharing a boat with the prince.
Humbled by his grace;
Not one bad word, or else I'll be humiliated.
My heart is endlessly troubled,
But to know the prince!
The mountain knows its trees, the tree knows its branches,
My heart delights in the prince, but he just doesn't know.

The Poem in a Nutshell

The 越人歌 is a poem from more than two thousand years ago, but it addresses a 21st century audience with both clarity and potency. It is a poem about love, but about love that can't be spoken. Love can't be spoken here because of the ways that politeness, considerateness and difference in social class or location actually get in the way of, rather than enable, intimate communication. In this poem, we have a prince and a person of unspecified social rank. The physical location is on a boat in mid-stream. Strong feelings are felt by the author, the invited guest, but these feelings can't be spoken.

Background

The poem appears in a collection of ancient stories put together in the 1st century BCE. The collector of these stories says the poem was originally written in the 6th century BCE in the State of Chu, in Southern China. Yet the original language of the poem was not Chinese, but was the language of the boatman who was singing this mesmerizing tune for his Chinese-speaking prince. The prince, overwhelmed by the beauty of the song, asked his attendant for a translation. Thus, one of the earliest Chinese love poems was not, in fact, written in Chinese. But because the 1st century BCE text preserves both the Chinese "translation" as well as the sounds of the original language, sounds that are represented in 32 Chinese characters, some modern scholars have tried to reconstruct the original, possibly Thai-based language of the poem. As of this date, those efforts are inconclusive, though highly suggestive.

One other brief observation: though the prince (王子) in the poem is a male, we are never told the gender of the other person. It is most natural to assume it is a woman who longs for the prince's attention and acknowledgment, but the text allows also a same-gender reading for both characters.

Analysis

This 54-character, ten-line poem records the exciting and even rapturous feelings of a person who has been invited aboard the prince's boat. The rhythmic nature of the poem is captured by the recurrent 兮 (xī), an untranslatable particle that serves to slow the action to allow maximum reflection. If we were to try to capture the 兮 with an English word, we might well say, "Ah" or "(Sigh)." As we read the poem aloud, we can almost hear the gentle movement of the boat as we intone the repeated 兮, which appears in the middle of each line. So memorable is that night, unforgettable really, to be privileged to share that special time with the prince (ll 1-4).

We aren't told whether the prince is attracted to the invitee or whether the prince is merely showing a kind of elegant politeness, but the resultant feeling in the one invited on the boat might best be called grateful vulnerability. The invitee is grateful because of the special access to the most influential person in the kingdom. Yet this gratitude also discloses vulnerability, described well in lines 5-6, a vulnerability that is captured between the words "humbled" and "humiliated." It is humbling to be invited to be with the prince (another translation has it: "The prince's kindness makes me shy"), but once the invitation has been accepted, the invitee becomes vulnerable to any whim of the prince. The humbled person can be humiliated by a gesture, a word, a glance or by being ignored. Once you are on the boat, you have to play by the prince's rules. Though we have given a clear sense to line 3, it is almost untranslatable, but that really is no obstacle to us. It is almost as if the thoughts are churning so deeply in the author's breasts that s/he can't quite get them out with clarity. "I am humbled; let me not be humiliated," is the sense.

The invitee would love to know the prince's true feelings, and the poem moves finally to that issue (ll 7-10). Does he love her? Or is he just demonstrating a refined and elegant civility? She, if we are allowed a specific gender reference, is clearly taken by his graciousness. Indeed, she adores (悦) him. But is the feeling reciprocal? Isn't it obvious that she cares deeply for the prince? Nature teaches us that trees in the mountains not only bear branches but know the branches. Why isn't it then the case that subjects of the prince, his true "branches," are known by the prince? Nature would lead us to believe that the prince *ought* to know the hearts of his subjects, the heart of the woman here. But he doesn't seem to. And, she can't tell him. She can't tell him because blurting out her love would wreck everything. The next move has to come from him. And, she just doesn't know his feelings towards her. And she can't ask.

唐

TANG DYNASTY

618-907 CE

相思
王维 | 唐

xiāng sī
wáng wéi táng

红豆生南国，
春来发几枝。
愿君多采撷，
此物最相思[1]。

hóng dòu shēng nán guó
chūn lái fā jǐ zhī
yuàn jūn duō cǎi xié
cǐ wù zuì xiāng sī

---

1 相思 – meaning to have lovesickness or nostalgic feelings; its meaning is diffi-
   cult to capture in a single word, though possible translations include "trigger,"
   "inspire," "stir," "elicit;" we selected "kindle" because of its connection with
   fire and redness

Longing
Wang Wei | Tang Dynasty

Red bean trees grow in the South,
Spring comes, they sprout new branches.
I hope you'll pick many,
They most kindle our love.

The Poem in a Nutshell

The heartfelt simplicity of this poem is forever etched in the minds of all students, not just of Chinese poetry, but of world literature. Wang Wei takes the most common of elements, the red bean, and builds his 20-character poem around it. Its red color was explained by a myth of a woman's tears, turning blood-red when she heard the news of the death of her husband in a border war and gushing over the beans. Ever thereafter, the red bean was a symbol of lovers separated, longing to return to each other's embrace.

Background

Along with Li Bai and Du Fu, Wang Wei (699-758) is considered one of the triad of the Tang Dynasty's greatest poets. But his accomplishments go far beyond poetry. A respected musician and landscape painter, he also occupied with distinction many official positions in the Chang'an-based government. His Buddhist commitments are evident in the simplicity of many of his poems. Captured in the An Lushan rebellion of the mid 750s, he was able to return to Chang'an and retire to his country residence on the Wang River, where he penned many poems.

Analysis

Song Dynasty poet Su Shi said about Wang Wei, "His poems can be summed as, they hold a painting within them." We see the truth of this upon reading these simple, but suggestive, 20 characters. A picture is drawn, of lovers separated, but of the desire of the author to be reminded to the beloved through the red beans. In understated fashion, the poet hopes that his beloved will gather many of those beans, for they both know of the beans, their love and the way their love is kindled through them.

While the simplicity and suggestiveness of the poem has often been mentioned, not as much noted has been how the middle character in each line functions to give the poem its penetrating directness. These four characters are 生, 发, 多, 最. They start us with "life" and bring us to "productivity" which leads to the desire to gather "many" of the beans. The gathering of the "many" will be the "most" evident proof of their undying love. Thus, the beans don't simply symbolize that love, but they as it were kindle it. The red color of the tear-stained beans, coupled with the ardent spirit of love, leads to a most powerful blaze of memory and longing.

长相思三首其一
李白 | 唐

cháng xiāng sī sān shǒu qí yī
lǐ bái tang

长相思，在长安。
络纬秋啼金井阑，
微霜凄凄¹簟色寒。
孤灯不明²思欲绝，
5 卷帷望月空长叹。

美人³如花隔云端⁴。

上有青冥之高天，
下有渌水之波澜。
天长路远⁵魂飞苦，
10 梦魂不到关山难。
长相思，摧心肝。

cháng xiāng sī zài cháng ān
luò wěi qiū tí jīn jǐng lán
wēi shuāng qī qī diàn sè hán
gū dēng bù míng sī yù jué
juàn wéi wàng yuè kōng cháng tàn

měi rén rú huā gé yún duān

shàng yǒu qīng míng zhī gāo tiān
xià yǒu lù shuǐ zhī bō lán
tiān cháng lù yuǎn hún fēi kǔ
mèng hún bù dào guān shān nán
cháng xiāng sī cuī xīn gān

---

1 凄凄 – used here to describe the chill of the night; the character brings a notion of bleakness to the scene

2 不明 – literally "not clear," "dim;" in this context it suggests also "不眠" which means "sleepless"

3 美人 – the one missed is a beautiful person; this is not reflected in the translation

4 云端 – a formal term for "high up in the clouds;" used in contemporary culture to refer to digital cloud storage systems

5 天长路远 – describing the long distance between them

25 Classic Chinese Love Poems

First of Three Poems to the Tune of "Longings"
Li Bai | Tang Dynasty

I am filled with longing to be in Chang'an.
Autumn crickets dolefully chirp on the golden well,
And a dusting of frost chills my bamboo mat.
Sleeplessly, by the lone lamp, I pine away,
I roll up the curtain, gaze at the distant moon, and sigh deeply.

You are like a flower far-off in the clouds.

Above is azure of the vast sky,
Below are the waves of the crystal-clear sea.
The arduous road wears down the spirit;
Even in my dreams, I can't cross the mountains that divide us.
I am filled with longing, and it breaks my heart.

The Poem in a Nutshell

In this moving poem by Li Bai, one of the Tang Dynasty's and China's greatest poets, we see tell-tale marks of his poetic genius. We *see* him first as a wanderer, away from the capital, the place of his beloved and the place of his former high position. We *hear* the chirping crickets; we *touch* the freezing sleeping mat; we *feel* his sense of utter bereavement as he looks longingly to the sky. Even the moon, which separated lovers know they share, can't bring him comfort. Their distance is unbridgeable, he can't change things, and it breaks his heart.

Background

Along with his friend and younger contemporary Du Fu, Li Bai (701-762) is considered the greatest of Tang Dynasty's accomplished poets, and among the most influential in Chinese history. His poems, 1000 of which still exist, are treasured by young and old. One of them, *Tranquil Night*, is among the first poems learned by Chinese children.

Yet his fame was certainly not assured from birth. Though born into an educated family in 701 and brought up in Sichuan, he declined to sit for the imperial exams when coming of age. Instead, he chose the life of an itinerant wanderer and poet. He married in his 20s and settled down for a while, with his poetry becoming honored, but he took to wandering again. He eventually ended up in Chang'an, the capital, where in 742 he was appointed by Emperor Xuanzong to be an inaugural member of the Hanlin Academy, an intellectual and literary circle charged with editing and commenting on the Confucian classics. Yet, the life of the wanderer may have been too deeply embedded in his heart; within two years he had offended the imperial host and was sent packing.

Analysis

Most think that this poem was written after his expulsion from Chang'an in 744. The poem describes both his deep longing for a woman left behind but also a yearning for that special intellectual fellowship and social position that he enjoyed in the capital. It reflects several features present in many of his other poems: a profound appreciation of nature, the ability to present a vivid picture in relatively simple language, and an awareness of the numbing realities of separation from those you love. In addition, the structure is neatly balanced, as if by structure itself the author is trying to combat the destabilizing feelings in his heart.

This poem, whose Chinese title means "Long Yearning," is the first and most famous in a trilogy of poems of separation. The poem has 11 neatly-balanced lines. Lines 1 and 11 mirror each other, with the only difference being that the yearning for Chang'an in line 1 becomes a yearning that breaks his heart in line 11. Longing or yearning encases the poem, surrounding all the other features of natural and emotional life.

The other nine lines neatly divide into lines 2-5 and 7-10, with line 6 functioning as both a link between sections and transition to the second section. The linking element in line 6 is 美人, literally "beautiful person," pointing to her—the reason for his poem in the first place. In the first section the poet deeply feels the isolation of his current situation. Loneliness often assails us in those quiet moments of the night where sleep flees and we are left alone in the dark with our thoughts. We see in our mind's eye the poet lying on his mat, hearing only the chirping of the autumn crickets (l 2). Note that the crickets gather on the "golden" well, a sign that his poverty of feeling isn't necessarily reflected in surroundings of deprivation.

The chill of the mat also prohibits sleeping. The lone lamp is losing its fight with the inky darkness. And so, he arises in the night, rolling up the curtain to gaze at the distant moon. The moon is *supposed* to unite separated lovers, since they both share the same moon, but all it does here is bring out a deep sigh.

His thoughts go to the clouds and beyond the clouds, where his beloved resides. His thoughts pass the sky and the undulating deep (ll 7-8), but then the reality of his situation assails him in lines 9-10. They are far away from each other. No amount of pining away; no amount of desire can change the unalterable fact that even his dreams can't cross the mountains that separate them (l 10). Ah, to be in Chang'an! Absence in this case doesn't make the heart grow fonder, as the English idiom has it. Rather, absence breaks his heart.

节妇吟寄东平李司空师道

张籍 | 唐

君知妾[1]有夫，
赠妾双明珠。
感君缠绵[2]意，
系在红罗襦[3]。

5　妾家高楼[4]连苑起，
良人执戟[5]明光里。
知君用心如日月[6]，
事夫誓拟同生死[7]。
还君明珠双泪垂，
10　恨不相逢未嫁时。

jié fù yín jì dōng píng lǐ sī kōng shī dào

zhāng jí táng

jūn zhī qiè yǒu fū
zèng qiè shuāng míng zhū
gǎn jūn chán mián yì
xì zài hóng luó rú

qiè jiā gāo lóu lián yuàn qǐ
liáng rén zhí jǐ míng guāng lǐ
zhī jūn yòng xīn rú rì yuè
shì fū shì nǐ tóng shēng sǐ
huán jūn míng zhū shuāng lèi chuí
hèn bù xiāng féng wèi jià shí

1　妾 – literally meaning concubine, but is in this case used as humble way for a married woman to refer to herself

2　缠绵 suggests a feeling of entanglement, of mutual affection

3　襦 – bodice of traditional outfit that is secured at the side with ties

4　高楼 – literally "high tower," possibly referring to the royal guards' quarters

5　执戟 – to hold a spear-like weapon called the Ji; emphasizes the husband's role as a guard

6　用心如日月 – the narrator compares the admirer's intentions to the sun and moon to show that they are clear and candid

7　同生死 – contrary to the Western vow of "till death do us part," this implies eternal connection both in life and in death

The Lament of the Faithful Wife Sent to His Excellency Li Shidao in Dongping County
Zhang Ji | Tang Dynasty

You know that I am married,
Yet you gave me a pair of shining pearls.
I feel your tender affection,
So I tied them on my red silk dress.

My home rises next to the royal garden,
My husband is a guard at the Bright Light Palace.
I know the purity of your intentions,
But I have already vowed eternal fidelity to my husband.
Weeping, I hereby return the pearls to you,
It breaks my heart that we didn't meet before I was married.

The Poem in a Nutshell

This poem focuses on a theme overlooked in most love poetry—the genuine interior struggle of a married woman who wishes she could turn the clock back and be free to explore love with a man who has sent her a gift. The mid-Tang Dynasty poet Zhang Ji presents this tension through the gift of a set of glittering pearls. The woman receives them, seemingly hesitates for a moment, and then ties them to her dress. But the reality of what she is doing dawns on her and she reluctantly, with tears, returns them. We see a simple movement of receiving and returning, but it is a deeply affecting movement.

Background

We know little of the mid-Tang Dynasty poet Zhang Ji (766-830). Until recently most Western readers only knew of him through one of his poems, a touching tribute to a friend apparently lost in battle on the Tibetan frontier, which was included in the famous anthology *300 Tang Poems* (Number 151). English readers are now in the debt of Prof. Jonathan Chaves, whose brilliant and diverse translations of 300 of Zhang Ji's poems (*Cloud Gate Song*, 2006) present the awesome diversity of Zhang Ji's poetry, from Music Bureau poems to evocative landscape depictions, as well as love poems.

Analysis

The subtitle of the poem suggests that it was sent to a military leader of the day, gently declining the offer of a position in his administration. Though reading this poem as both a political and love poem highlights its literary genius, here we focus on it as a love poem. If we read it that way, we quickly conclude it is a touching and sincere reflection on love that cannot be consummated. Its title is 节妇吟, The Lament of the Faithful Wife, and its content neatly breaks down into two stanzas of unequal length. The first stanza consists of four lines, each of five characters; the second has six lines, but each with seven characters.

In the first stanza (ll 1-4), the author faces what one might call a joyful dilemma. She receives the unexpected gift of a pair of shining pearls. Under normal circumstances this would be a reason for celebration, but she is married and she knows that the sender of the gift is not her husband. Yet, impressed by the gift, she attaches it to her dress as a constant visual reminder of the thoughtfulness of a friend. That she is clearly torn by the gift can be seen by the first words of the entire poem: "You know that I am married." How does she say these words? With fierce indignation? In gentle protest? With secret admiration of the giver?

The first stanza presents a very private reflection. We readers are privileged to join the speaker in her interior space as she weighs what kind of present she actually has received. Keeping the question ever before her are the two shimmering pearls that glitter on her dress.

25 Classic Chinese Love Poems

But her internal soliloquy of the first stanza must move to the exterior places of life, since she isn't a woman alone in the world, without connection or relationships. Almost as if waking from a pleasant dream, she plunges into the reality of her current life in lines 5-10. Line 5 talks about home and line 6 about her husband, her two social anchors in the world, anchors that destabilize the shimmering lure of the pearls. She confesses she is a woman of prominence, residing adjacent to the royal hunting garden. Her husband is in the royal guard. She has location and identity in the world.

The tension never leaves her heart. On the one hand the giver can be trusted; his intentions are pure (l 7). But how do we know that she isn't engaging in a pleasant act of self-deception? Men don't often shower presents on married women for no apparent reason. Her resolve seems strong, as she reaffirms her commitment to her husband. Our translation of line 9 ("I hereby return") is meant to capture the almost legal nature of her decision. Torn in heart but knowing what is right, she returns the pearls.

But she can't help but wondering, "What if...? What if we had met long ago? What if life had been different?" The endless cycle of regret and of wishing for alternative paths stays with her even as she wraps her tear-stained poem around the shining pearls and sends them back.

离思五首其四
元稹 | 唐

曾经沧海难为水，[1]
除却巫山不是云。
取次花丛懒回顾，
半缘修道半缘君。[2]

lí sī wǔ shǒu qí sì
yuán zhěn tang

céng jīng cāng hǎi nán wéi shuǐ
chú què wū shān bù shì yún
qǔ cì huā cóng lǎn huí gù
bàn yuán xiū dào bàn yuán jūn

---

1 There is no verb in this line but a sense of yearning is implied

2 Other English translations pick up on the "半" and tend to give a "half-and-half" rendering, but we read it as a full commitment to both Dao and the person in the narrator's heart

Fourth of Five Poems of Departure
Yuan Zhen | Tang Dynasty

I cannot yearn for lesser waters once I have seen the deep blue sea,
In comparison to Wu Mountain's clouds, all others have no color.
I stroll past fields of flowers, not giving them a second glance,
Because my heart is in the Dao, and you are in my heart.

The Poem in a Nutshell

In this poem Yuan Zhen provides a simple, clear, unforgettable picture of the pain of lost love and the desire to be faithful to the one who has died. We might in the West say that a lost loved one provided an anchor of stability. In contrast, Yuan Zhen talks about her as an incomparably beautiful natural feature—the deep blue sea or the cloud-shrouded Wu Mountain. Yet life goes on, and she remains in his heart while he is faithful to both the Way (the Dao) and to her. He has one love but two incandescent sources of light.

Background

Yuan Zhen (779-831) was a mid-Tang Dynasty government official, poet and author of what some have characterized as the first modern "novel" in Chinese history, the *Yingying Zhuan* or "Story of Yingying." He developed a friendship with the famed minister-poet Bai Juyi, and together they made plans to retire to the countryside to live simply and further develop their poetic skills. Yet Yuan Zhen's comparatively early death (at age 52) precluded that from happening.

He met and married 韦丛, the love of his life, in his early 20s. After seven blissful years, she fell ill and died, leaving him with a broken heart but a sharp pen. Over the next few years he composed several love poems, reflecting both on their relationship and the yawning emotional gulf that resulted from her passing. Our poem is the fourth of five poems in his series named 离思, "Thoughts on Departure." Each of the five describes different aspects of their relationship. This one focuses quite simply on her incomparability.

Analysis

The formal structure of this poem is a 绝句, in this case a quatrain of seven-syllable lines. It unfolds one idea in an ever-more moving fashion, ending with a line that not only summarizes the development of the idea but does so in an arresting and memorable fashion. The main theme is his departed wife's uniqueness, a uniqueness that makes other possible love targets no more interesting than typical flowers.

Lines 1 and 2 capture her uniqueness and incomparability by contrasting unforgettable natural features with lesser features of the same type. Once seeing the vast expanse of ocean, one isn't entranced with a river or lake. Once witnessing the mysterious enveloping clouds of Wu Mountain, other clouds seem like so many puffs of white. Though few would argue that the clouds surrounding Wu Mountain in the south are uniquely different than other clouds, the poet gives us what we might call the "geography of imagination" or a "geography of seductive allure" that makes us look at the common river or cloud as bordering on the insignificant.

Other women hold no allure for the poet (l 3). He passes through the "flower bushes" (花丛) without looking back. He chooses the phrase 花丛, the second character of which is his beloved's name, but instead of a "flower" bush her actual name is *wei* bush. Homophonous with her name is 伟, which means "big" or "great." The rest are "flower" bushes, while she is the "really huge" bush. Unlike a later poem in this collection (page 89), where the poet turns around and finds his true love, in this case the poet doesn't even turn. He knows that he has experienced the best.

The final line is unexpectedly rich. Twice appearing is the character 半, usually rendered "half." Most other English translations so render it ("half with the Dao and half with you") but the effect of "half" with the Dao and "half" with her gives the poem a kind of split allegiance which contradicts the essential emotion of the poem. Now that she is gone, the poet has to occupy his time and he occupies it with the Way, the Dao. Yet she is never far from his mind even in his deepest study. Thus, though the line literally says "because half is the Dao and half is you," the meaning is that he is fully *in both*. He finds her in the Dao and the Dao in her. He enjoys both, and is continually nourished by both. We should all be so fortunate.

题都城南庄[1]
崔护 | 唐

去年今日此门中，
人面桃花相映红。
人面[2]不知何处去，
桃花依旧笑春风。

tí dū chéng nán zhuāng
cuī hù táng

qù nián jīn rì cǐ mén zhōng
rén miàn táo huā xiāng yìng hóng
rén miàn bù zhī hé chù qù
táo huā yī jiù xiào chūn fēng

---

1 题 – in poetry, translated as "in memory of"; "on" is a neutral translation

2 人面 – literally "the face" or "human face," which we have translated "pretty face," holds the same position in lines 2 and 3

On the South Manor of the Capital City
Cui Hu | Tang Dynasty

Last year, on this very day, at this very gate,
That pretty face and the peach blossom mirrored each other's blush.
I just don't know where that pretty face went,
But the peach blossom, as always, smiles in spring breeze.

The Poem in a Nutshell

This poem beguiles us by its apparent simplicity and transparency. In two straightforward scenes the author describes his visit to the identical spot on the identical day one year apart. On the first visit he met a young woman, whose rose-hued face mirrored the brilliant reds of the peach tree blossoms. On the second visit he just saw the peach tree, beautiful as the previous year, but the enchanting woman wasn't there. Our first reaction might be, "Well, that is unfortunate," but as we read and re-read the poem, its simplicity becomes transformed in our minds into a kind of drama of human life, where we meet and lose perhaps even the potential love of our lives because life and circumstances simply change.

Background

In 28 simple characters, none of them complex or obscure, this poem works its way into our heart and won't let us go. The circumstances of its composition and even the historicity of its author are widely debated. First appearing in a mid-ninth century Tang Dynasty poetic anthology, 本事诗 (Storied Poems), the poem already then had a rich and melodramatic story associated with it. On a cool Qingming Day in the Tang Dynasty, a young man (Cui Hu), who had just failed the imperial examination, happened upon a home south of the capital of Chang'an. Thirsty and weary, he knocked on the door. It was opened by a beautiful young lady, with whom he immediately fell in love. After quenching his thirst, he left, planning to return the next year. But when he came back no one was home, and so he penned this poem on the wall and left. A few days later he returned, to be greeted by her father, who sadly informed Cui Hu that his daughter had just died of lovesickness after reading the words etched on the wall. She, too, had fallen in love, and had thought she would never see him again. Her body was still lying on her bed inside. When Cui Hu entered and saw her, he whispered, "I'm here! I'm here!" and she miraculously returned to life. In gratitude, the father gave his daughter to be married to Cui Hu.

Analysis

Though we almost chuckle because of the perfectly unlikely ending of this story, we see, if we think about it for a minute, that the very silence in the poem encourages readers to add additional details, compose a story and, in fact, put their own life into the 28 brief characters of the poem. We can imagine a distraught young man, thinking that his life or at least his career prospects were dashed after failing the exam, wearily seeking a simple courtesy by knocking on a door. We can imagine that in this condition almost *any* young woman would have struck him as inordinately beautiful and able to make his life meaningful. We can imagine reticence and unwillingness to reveal initial feelings; the decision to return again; the overwrought emotions in finding that she was not there; the plaintive and resigned calling card of this poem etched on the wall; the fatal effect on the young lady (in this case a

15-year-old girl). We can imagine all of these things emerging from the simple and transparent clarity of the two stanzas.

The poem is told from the standpoint of "today," but the first stanza describes the author's visit to a place south of the Capital just a year before "today." In a particular spot on a memorable day he recalled the brilliant red of the peach blossoms and how they reflected the ruddy purity and beauty of a young female. There was a kind of mutuality (相) in the reflection; a sense that perfection was manifest right before his eyes.

The second stanza describes the same place on the same day one year later. The red of the peach blossoms remained, but she was gone. No one knew where she went, but only the brilliant peach remains "as before" (依旧). So little has changed really but because the object of desire is not there, everything in fact has changed.

The poem delights us because of its quiet suggestiveness. We know the excitement of discovering, perhaps unexpectedly, a beautiful or handsome person and the deep impression it makes upon us. Often that impression is reinforced by some feature of the person that is unforgettable: the eyes, a gesture, the shape of the body, the words exchanged. We depart, probably not saying everything our heart tells us to say because we are afraid that our emotions might take over and reduce us to becoming a fool or an incoherent speaker. So, we withdraw, unaware of the effect of the person on our heart and us on their heart. But then, we relive the meeting, trying to interpret and reinterpret every word and gesture. Does the person think of me as I of her or him? I have to return! But then, on return, all things are the same, except the person has gone. Life often doesn't give us the gift of bringing the beloved back to life; often all that is left is the wisp of a memory, and the lovesick longing for a relationship and a person that briefly flitted across our life's landscape. Nature continues with its beautiful colors but, somehow, the human colors are muted as we add sorrow to our catalogue of words well-learned.

新添声杨柳枝词二首其二

xīn tiān tang tang liǔ zhī cí èr shǒu qí èr

温庭筠 | 唐

wēn tang yún tang

井底点灯深烛¹伊，
共郎长行莫围棋²。
玲珑骰子安红豆³，
入骨相思知不知?

jǐng dǐ diǎn dēng shēn zhú yī
gòng láng cháng xíng mò wéi qí
líng lóng tóu zǐ ān hóng dòu
rù gǔ xiāng sī zhī bù zhī

---

1 深烛 – literally "deep candle;" here the 烛 stands for 嘱, which means to urge; this is the first of several homophonic wordplays that define the poem

2 长行莫围棋 – 长行 and 围棋 are two games popular in the Tang Dynasty, Long Journey and Go. The narrator asks her lover not to play Go, which is an intellectually demanding game that often takes many hours, even days, to play. The pronunciation of of the game Go (wéi qí) is homophonous with the word 违期 (wéi qī), literally to not violate the time or not delay the return, which is captured in our translation . In contrast, she urges him to play Long Journey, a Tang era game distinguished by its use of dice and characterized by quick rounds.

3 红豆 – red beans; symbol of love and longing; immortalized in Wang Wei's poem, "Longing" (page 29)

Second of Two Poems to the Tune of the Song of the Willow with New Sounds Added

Wen Tingyun | Tang Dynasty

A lantern shines in a well. I deeply urge you
Not to delay your return, because my heart is with you on this long journey.
The red dots set in the exquisite dice are red beans of love,
Don't you know that my love is just as deeply-rooted?

The Poem in a Nutshell

Chinese love poetry often uses images drawn from nature or the heavenly bodies to express feelings of longing, loss and love. In contrast, this poem uses two unexpected methods to explore love. First is word play. Because the Chinese language has a more limited range of sounds than many other languages, many words sound the same; even more have the same spelling, though differing in tone. This poem plays on words—several times. Second is likening a love relationship to ancient board games, and especially to the dice used in them. What results is a fresh and ingenious look at love.

Background

For most of the past 1000 years, the late Tang Dynasty poet Wen Tingyun (798-866?) has been appreciated for his colorful lyrics and intimate portraits of the interior life of women. Generally, however, he has been seen as a poet not engaged with the society around him and thus a rather inferior representative of late Tang Dynasty poetry. Yet, a reevaluation is underway. In his 1998 dissertation, published in 2004, Huaichuan Mou argues that a deep consideration of the poet's life reveals insight into his sometimes-tangled words but also gives fresh insight into his engagement with the era in which he lived.

Analysis

Our poem is only 28 characters, and we are immediately confused by the first line. What is the connection between a lantern shining in a well and the author's urging her lover not to put off his return to her? It is all in the sounds of words. The first line literally reads, "Deep in a well shines a lantern; deep candle you." But the last words don't make sense, of course, and the poet wants us use the character 烛 (zhú), translated "candle," to encourage us to think about other words spelled "zhu" to give the intended meaning. It happens that 嘱 (zhǔ) means "to enjoin" or "to urge." If we go through that mental process, realizing that the author is interested in homophones rather than literal meanings, we have the key to the poem.

Now that the author's method is clear, we see two more homophones in line 2. But these are not just clever word plays; they give meaning to the poem. She wants to be in his heart on his "long trip" and then "not 围棋" or not "Go (the game)." But the game Go, written *wei qi* in Chinese, sounds exactly the same (though tones are different) to 违期 (wéi qī) "don't violate/offend/delay the time." The meaning then, when the second phrase is allowed, is "I am with you on your long journey, don't delay your return."

But something even more subtle is going on. The words "long journey" (长行) are also the name of a Tang Dynasty board game, played with dice. Unlike Go, which was an intellectual's game, and often took many hours or even days to complete, 长行 was a popular game that was quickly over. The author is saying, through the medium of two board games, that she hopes her lover plays the quickly-over "Long Journey" game rather than the slow "Go" game. Play the *short* game, not the *long* game. Come back soon! No more ingenious method of expressing her longing could be imagined.

But there is more. Line three describes the dice used in the games, and notes that its red dots can be called 红豆, "red love beans." This was the phrase immortalized by Wang Wei (699-758) in the poem discussed above. These are the beans that most trigger nostalgic feelings of a lover who is away. So for Wen Tingyun, even the exquisitely carved dice scream out love!

The final line likens the poet's love to these red "love bean dice." But to be noted is the opening phrase: 入骨. Literally this means "in the bones." We have the phrase to "love someone to the bones" and that would be faithful to the meaning. But even more significant is that the technology of dice changed about the time the poem was written: originally they were made of jade, but then it changed into bone...or 入 ("into") 骨 ("bone").

If you had been the recipient of this enormously clever and heartfelt poem, don't you think you would have hightailed it home as quickly as possible?

锦瑟
李商隐 | 唐

锦瑟无端五十弦[1]，
一弦一柱思华年[2]。
庄生晓[3]梦迷蝴蝶，
望帝春心托杜鹃。
沧海月明珠有泪，[4]
蓝田[5]日暖玉生烟。
此情可待成追忆，
只是当时已惘然。

jǐn sè
lǐ shāng yǐn tang

jǐn sè wú duān wǔ shí xián
yī xián yī zhù sī huá nián
zhuāng shēng xiǎo mèng mí hú dié
wàng dì chūn xīn tuō dù juān
cāng hǎi yuè míng zhū yǒu lèi
lán tián rì nuǎn yù shēng yān
cǐ qíng kě dài chéng zhuī yì
zhī shì dāng shí yǐ wǎng rán

---

1 Traditional zithers generally had 25 strings; thus the 50-stringed zither in this poem seems to be wuduan (for no reason). Yet, according to an ancient story told in our essay, an emperor was so moved by a goddess's playing that he broke his zither, thus a 50 stringed zither is a symbol of heartbreak.

2 华年 – literally "glorious years," youth is associated with glory and prosperity

3 晓 – character for "morning," but in this case is an abbreviation for 知晓, meaning "to know"

4 In Chinese culture as well as many others, mermaids' tears are sought after by seafarers as pearls or elixirs; a Chinese myth in antiquity mentions such creatures whose tears turn into pearl

5 蓝田 - Lantian mountains, located in Lantian county, known for its jade reserve

Zither
Li Shangyin | Tang Dynasty

Why does this exquisite zither have 50 strings?
Each string and bridge reminds me of my youth.
Mr. Zhuang, lost in his dreams, turns into a butterfly,
Emperor Wang's amorous spring heart is bequeathed to the cuckoo.
On the blue sea, in the bright moonlight, the mermaids shed tears of pearl.
In the mountains, under the warm sun, the jade becomes smoke.
This feeling, now, has grown into a memory,
But at that time, I was utterly lost.

The Poem in a Nutshell

As previously mentioned, most Tang-era poets attained their status because of their ability to use nature and natural phenomena to produce clear and lasting images in the minds of readers. In contrast, this poem by Li Shangyin both delights and challenges us because of the obscurity but lush suggestiveness of the imagery. Here the poet indulges in sensuous ruminations, calling on the story of Zhuangzi to probe the real vs the imagined and the story of Emperor Wang to lament lost love. His reference to a story of mermaid tears alludes to the idea of ambition lost. Finally, the jade becoming smoke indicates that even things that appear clear at a distance disappear upon closer inspection. Memory could have been such a positive companion but, in the end, it compounds the poet's feeling of alienation and confusion.

Background

Li Shangyin (813-858) lived during the declining years of the Tang Dynasty. Gone were the days of bold national expansion, of celebratory palace dances and expressions of wealth, of the work of dozens of poets whose lyrics are still quoted by child and adult alike. In its place was factionalism, palace intrigue, multiple power centers and continuous turmoil. Engagement in contemporary political struggles would most likely have endangered one's career, but withdrawal from the struggles would have left one on the sidelines. In this confusing time a new poetry of interiority and dense allusiveness, captured brilliantly in this poem, emerged. Richly nuanced historical and mythical allusions are surrounded by images of confusion or illusion. Even though perplexity seems to result, the poem beckons to us to try to understand both the events referred to and the overwhelming sense of confusion that accompanies the poet in his later years.

Analysis

In 56 well-chosen characters, Li Shangyin takes us on a tumultuous journey of rejection and bewilderment. The first 14 characters reflect on the exquisite zither and its sad tune; the next 28 characters explore the themes of illusion and reality, while the last 14 characters speak of the contrast between the memory formed of earlier life events and the confusion felt while having lived through the events themselves. Altogether it adds up to a plaintive poem of regret—especially of lost love and ambition—with the final word of the poem being 惘然, confusion or perplexity.

The classical zither didn't have a fixed number of strings, but most ancient treatments of it speak of it as having 25 strings. An ancient story tells of a ruler who heard a young girl playing on the 25-string zither, and he was so moved to sadness by its heart-rending sound that he broke it in two—thus making it a 50-string zither. When our author opens with reference to a 50-string zither, then, we are to think of this story and to see in the reference to a 50-string zither a sign that what follows is "doubly sad."

The heart of the poem (the 28 middle-characters) turns to stories that illumine the days of his youth. First up is a reference to the famous story in Zhuangzi where he was perplexed whether he became a butterfly in his dream or the butterfly became Zhuangzi. That story is included as a signal to the reader that the poem will bring us into a world of illusion and unclarity. What is real, anyway? How is the past real? Is it simply a dream, with no substantial existence? But then, after presenting that issue, he turns to two stories, one about lost love and one of lost ambition.

In the first, Emperor Wang turns into a cuckoo. Many scholars believe this refers to an imperial figure of old who had designs on the wife of one of his subordinates. The emperor transferred this imperial figure so as to give him free access to his target. Later, however, he was overwhelmed by his guilt and, when he died, was said to have been transformed into a cuckoo bird, which called out miserably all night until blood flowed from the bird's throat. A reasonable inference is that the author tells this story because he, too, lost love and is filled with the remorse and perhaps even guilt because of that lost love.

In the second story, we may have an allusion to the common belief that mermaids, when weeping, shed tears. Yet, behind this commonplace observation stands a 成语 or idiom, 沧海遗珠 (cāng hǎi yí zhū), which is translated as "a leftover pearl in the depth of the sea," and has been interpreted as an idiom of talent unappreciated and unused. This, then, would be how the poet felt. The final seven characters of this middle section again take up the idea of illusion vs reality. When one climbs Indigo Mountain, the thing that at first seems clear (jade) is swallowed up in a dense smoke.

All of these memories now come back to him (last 14 characters), but he can't really enjoy the pleasure of these memories because, as he experienced the events, he was in a fog; he was lost. Thus, rather than sharpness and pleasure we are left with unbearable sadness and a sense of loss—of love and talent unappreciated. By honoring the richly-textured poem today, we are finally able to give Li Shangyin some of the honor he thought perished with him.

陇西行其二
陈陶 | 唐

誓扫匈奴[1]不顾身，
五千貂锦丧胡尘[2]。
可怜无定河边骨，
犹是春闺梦里人。

shì sǎo xiōng nú bù gù shēn
wǔ qiān diāo jǐn sāng hú chén
kě lián wú dìng hé biān gǔ
yóu shì chūn guī mèng lǐ rén

---

1 匈奴 – Xiongnu, also known in the West as the Huns, were a fierce nomadic people who inhabited parts of current Inner Mongolia, Siberia, Gansu, and Xinjiang

2 尘 – dust; this line is reminiscent of the colloquial English expression, "bite the dust," though we present the more elegant English translation, "perish in the desert"

Second Poem of Military Expedition to Longxi County
Chen Tao | Tang Dynasty

They swore on their lives to wipe out the Xiongnu,
Five thousand mink-clad elite troops perished in the desert.
It's a pity these soldiers, bones strewn by the Wuding River,
Appear in their lovers' boudoir dreams.

The Poem in a Nutshell

In 28 brief characters, late Tang Dynasty poet Chen Tao creates a memorable picture of an unsuccessful attempt of elite troops to ward off northern invaders. What makes the poem unforgettable is not the battle itself—those are quite common—but the way Chen Tao contrasts the martial spirit of the troops, their complete defeat, and the deceptive dreams in the minds of the deceased troops' wives. The wives haven't received news from their husbands; they "see" them in their dreams as happy and strong. In fact, their bodies are strewn along the Wuding River. An utter pity.

Background

By the time Chen Tao (824-882) wrote this poem, the glory days of the Tang Dynasty were just about over. Continuous harassment by northern enemies, here called the "Xiong Nu" or "Huns," combined with internal conflict within the empire led to vulnerability and eventually the collapse of the Tang. This poem is particularly worthy of fresh translation because of its prominent position in the first great work of Chinese poetry translated into English, the 1920 volume *Three Hundred Tang Poems* (number 309). We don't know a lot about Chen Tao. Unlike many prominent poets, he didn't have an official government appointment. After his study in the capital, he lived a rather itinerant life, spending a long period living as an impoverished recluse.

Analysis

This poem is drenched in sadness and pity. The first 14 characters describe the sadness and the second 14 characters present the pity. It is not as if the poem and military expedition which it describes started out being sad. In contrast, the massing of 5000 elite Tang Dynasty troops heading off to the north to fight the barbarian foe was no doubt attended with all kinds of demonstrations of loyalty and good wishes for a successful fight. The first line captures a little of that spirit. The men swore that they would fight to the death to defeat this northern menace. 誓扫, the opening phrase, is literally translated "swear to sweep up..." i.e., in language familiar to us today we might say that the men swore to "clean up" or "wipe out" or "wipe the floor with" their vicious enemies in the north. We can imagine the manly confidence and bravado in a stirring departure ceremony. Musical instruments, solemn pledges, festive uniforms—all of these conspired to give the impression of invincibility.

But things didn't turn out that way. Line 2 brings us back to the harsh reality—all 5000 of the elite and brightly adorned troops ended up dead. Instead of lively marching bodies, we have scattered corpses. The language of line 2 brings up the stark contrast between the richness of the "mink-clad" or "sable/marten-clad" troops and the humiliation of nothing but "bones" (骨) lying by the river.

The sadness of these lines is then complemented by pity in the final two lines. Line 3 begins with that word (可怜, "What a pity!"). Though the author never enumerates these pities separately, we have a three-fold pity in these lines. First, it is a pity that the soldiers perished. The finest of a fine generation dying on the battlefield is always reason for sympathetic feelings.

But the larger pity is for the wives, described in line 4. They have to remain behind while their courageous husbands are at war. They receive no mail, no communication from their husbands, perhaps for a few years. What are they to think? They imagine various scenarios, no doubt, but they also feel their husbands are safe, winning wars for the Tang. They see their husbands in their dreams, and the husbands they see are the vigorous and energetic men that went to war. It's a pity that they don't know the truth but that they had to continue to live their lives in fantasyland.

Finally, the third pity is on the reader. We feel strangely moved not just by the scene of scattered corpses and hopeful wives, but also by the fact that we, the reader, are the only ones that know the truth of the matter. We as it were "see" the battle happening; we "see" each wife in her boudoir dreaming the pleasant dreams about her husband. We know that everything has gone wrong. But we can do nothing about it but pity everyone.

The poem is also memorable because of the final character of each line. The first and fourth lines end with 身 ("body") and 人 ("man/person"). The men are vigorously alive. But the second and third lines end with 尘 ("dust") and 骨 ("bones"). Regrettably, lines 2 and 3 tell the real story of this sad poem.

君生我未生，我生君已老

jūn shēng wǒ wèi sheng wǒ shēng jūn yǐ lǎo

佚名 | 唐

yì míng táng

君生我未生，	jūn shēng wǒ wèi shēng
我生君已老。	wǒ shēng jūn yǐ lǎo
君恨¹我生迟，	jūn hèn wǒ shēng chí
我恨君生早。	wǒ hèn jūn shēng zǎo
5　君生我未生，	jūn shēng wǒ wèi shēng
我生君已老。	wǒ shēng jūn yǐ lǎo
恨不生同时，	hèn bù shēng tóng shí
日日与君好。	rì rì yǔ jūn hǎo
²我生君未生，	wǒ shēng jūn wèi shēng
10　君生我已老。	jūn shēng wǒ yǐ lǎo
我离君天涯，	wǒ lí jūn tiān yá
君隔我海角³。	jūn gé wǒ hǎi jiǎo
我生君未生，	wǒ shēng jūn wèi shēng
君生我已老。	jūn shēng wǒ yǐ lǎo
15　⁴化蝶去寻花，	huà dié qù xún huā
夜夜栖芳草。	yè yè qī fāng cǎo

1　恨 has a wide range of meanings including "hate, despise, regret," and "grieve;" we have rendered it as "It's a shame" to express the narrator's powerlessness in this situation

2　In the second stanza, the speaker is the older person

3　天涯海角 – idiom meaning "the ends of the earth," is split between lines 11 and 12, paralleling the separation of the lovers. We have rendered it here as "worlds apart" to show the figurative distance between the lovers

4　There is no subject in this line, but we interpreted it as a wish by both parties to be together

I Was Not Yet Born When You Were Born, Once I Was Born, You Were Already Old
Unknown | Tang Dynasty

I was not yet born when you were born,
Once I was born, you were already old.
It's a shame that I was born so late,
And you were born so early.
I was not yet born when you were born,
Once I was born, you were already old.
It's a shame that we weren't born at the same time,
Then I would gladly be with you every day.

You were not yet born when I was born,
Once you were born, I was already old.
I am worlds apart from you,
As you are from me.
You were not yet born when I was born,
Once you were born, I was already old.
If only we were butterflies, we'd dance among the flowers,
And every night we would rest on the fragrant grass.

The Poem in a Nutshell

This famous poem explores the problem of mismatched lovers. There are so many ways that mismatches happen between lovers—social class distinctions, religious differences, intelligence or personality contrasts, but our poem explores the notion of age mismatch. We might tend to chuckle at this—age rarely seems to be an obstacle to couples connecting. Yet, in this poem from the Tang Dynasty, the stark contrast between a younger and much older lover means that their love can never happen this side of the grave. A gentle remonstrance and wish for eternal happiness together is all that is left for the lovers.

Background

The neatly balanced rhythms and repeated refrains of this Tang Dynasty anonymous love poem cannot hide the fact that the lovers face an insuperable obstacle to consummating their love. That obstacle is stated in the first ten characters: "I was not yet born when you were born, and by the time i was born, you were old." While many in the West might shrug shoulders and say, "If it is truly love, age is no obstacle," the same was not true in Tang Dynasty China. Early marriages between young people of like age were the norm, indeed the requirement. The future of the civilization depended on it.

Yet, love works its strange ways among humans. There is often a mutuality between very young and much older people. It might start innocently enough—with playing of games, giving of presents, hugs and kisses and other signs of mutual endearment— but then something happens, and the very young and the much older person fall in love.

When a culture doesn't permit these kind of relations to mature into a marriage connection, much like the culture of Verona in Shakespeare's play *Romeo and Juliet* didn't allow their love to be licit, lovers are faced with enormous challenges. Do you try to circumvent the rules? Live within the societal strictures but complain?

Analysis

Our poem explores this idea in two ways: 1) by lamenting the limitations on the couple; and 2) by wishing for a day of release when the relationship can be consummated. The last line of the poem mentions this idea by hinting at one of the most noted love stories of Chinese history—that of Liang Shanbo and Zhu Yingtai.

The lamentation of this poem is rhythmic, balanced and apparently controlled. Of the sixteen lines of the poem, lines 5-6 repeat lines 1-2, and lines 13-14 repeat lines 9-10. Lines 1-8 are placed in the mouth of one of the couple, and lines 9-16 are spoken by the other. The problem, therefore, is stated four times: one is not born when the other was alive, and by the time the one is born, the other is already old. Each of the partners says this, from his or her perspective, twice.

Half of the poem, then, speaks the most basic, straightforward and inescapable truth. Mismatch in age.

The other eight lines give us an insight into the depth of the emotion felt by the seemingly unemotional and rhythmic chanting of lines 1-2, 5-6, 9-10, and 13-14. Line 3-4 use an all-purpose "hate" word (恨 – "hate, despise, regret, grieve") to describe just how bad this situation is. One can shake fists at heaven or lose oneself in tears, but the authors here content themselves with the deeply emotional "It is just such a shame that…."

Lines 7-8 describe their wish: to have been born at the same time and to spend their days together. But lines 11-12 and 15-16 take us in new directions. The former recognizes that there are profound differences between the two. They are "worlds apart," and the reader is left to imagine the nature of that difference, whether it is geographical, cultural or experience difference.

But then, as if trying to pull triumph out of a lost situation, the poet concludes with a wish in lines 15-16: that they both become butterflies, night after night perching on the same fragrant grass, day after day flitting to the same flowers. This last wish can best be understood in the context of the love story, first attested in the Eastern Jin Dynasty (3rd-5th centuries CE), where Liang Shanbo and Zhu Yingtai (disguised as a boy) were sent off to school in Hangzhou, and they gradually developed deep affection for one another. But the girl was called home to be married to a local merchant, against her wishes. This contributed to her boyfriend's gradual loss of health and eventual death. As she was going to her marriage celebration, her procession passed by his grave, which opened up, swallowed her, and then produced two butterflies—the lovers who would then be inseparable forever.

We smile at the simplicity of the story, but are moved nevertheless by the profound reflection, in very simple words, on the enduring conundrum of mismatches in love.

宋

SONG DYNASTY

960-1279 CE

蝶恋花二首其一
欧阳修 | 宋

庭院深深深[1]几许？
杨柳堆烟，帘幕无重数.
玉勒雕鞍游冶处[2]，
楼高不见章台路[3]。

雨横风狂三月暮，
门掩黄昏，无计留春住。
泪眼问花花不语，
乱红飞过秋千去[4]。

dié liàn huā èr shǒu qí yī
ōu song xiū song

tíng yuàn shēn shēn shēn jǐ xǔ
yáng liǔ duī yān lián mù wú chóng shù
yù lè diāo ān yóu yě chù
lóu gāo bù jiàn zhāng tái lù

yǔ hèng fēng kuáng sān yuè mù
mén yǎn huáng hūn wú jì liú chūn zhù
lèi yǎn wèn huā huā bù yǔ
luàn hóng fēi guò qiū qiān qù

---

1 The use of three consecutive 深 (deep) suggests a feeling of isolated confinement

2 He rode off to a brothel

3 Literally "I can't see the Zhangtai Road," which is another euphemism for the brothel mentioned in the previous line

4 Literally "the red flowers fly past the swings," but our translation emphasizes they, like he, fly away

First of Two Poems to the Tune of "Butterfly Loves Flowers"
Ouyang Xiu | Song Dynasty

So so deep in the courtyard, so so deep.
Surrounded by a thick fog of willows, forming layer upon layer of curtains.
On a horse with jade bit and carved saddle, he rode off,
I climb the tower but see no trace of him.

Driving rain and violent wind mark the end of March.
I close the doors at dusk, powerless to make the Spring stay.
I tearfully ask the flowers, but the flowers don't speak,
Rather, in a blur of red, they fly away too.

The Poem in a Nutshell

This poem by the multi-talented early Song Dynasty's Ouyang Xiu is technically known as a 闺怨 (guī yuàn), the lament of a woman confined to her boudoir. Though she may have all the trappings of aristocratic life, she lacks the one thing that she most longs for: a husband who treasures her alone. Instead, while he is off riding to the brothel, she mounts the steps of her tower, wordlessly scanning the horizon for him. He isn't there; he has gone. The last words of the poem, where beautiful flowers drift away, capture her dual feelings of powerlessness and abandonment.

Background

The life of Ouyang Xiu (1007-72) reflects the Chinese cultural ideal of the scholarly civil servant. Throughout his life he held high military and civil positions in the Song Dynasty, but he also used those positions to further his own skills in poetry and history writing, calligraphy and painting. His historical works on the Tang Dynasty and the political upheaval in the Five Dynasty period of the 10th century used the traditional Confucian values of loyalty and benevolence to judge the effectiveness of historical figures. His poetic style also reflected a desire to return to what was considered a simpler literary form, abandoning what some have called the "mannered and excessively rhythmic style" then popular.

But as with almost every reformer in history, his opinions encountered opposition. He was thrown out of office, became a roving poet and painter, and was recalled to the capital where he led the movement for reform of the Civil Service exams along Confucian lines. History now knows him as one of the eight Great Masters of the Tang/Song Dynasty (唐宋八大家之一).

Analysis

This engaging poem is traditionally known as a "bourdoir lament," or a description of the feelings of a woman confined to her home while her husband is away either on state service or, as here, on other romantic dalliances. Though it reflects the feelings of a heartbroken woman who expresses an awareness of her powerless position, it is written with balanced lines and clear meaning.

The first four lines describe her isolated situation, and the last four present the emotions attendant on that situation. The pivotal middle line gives the reason that links the isolation with the emotions: her husband can't be seen as she mounts the tower to look for him. He is off cavorting with courtesans, leaving her in her emotional desolation.

We begin with the unforgettable triple appearance of the word "deep" (深) in line 1. That word captures both her sense of confinement or even imprisonment in her home and courtyard as well as perhaps an indication that she secretly longs for what is even "deeper"—the grave. As we intone each successive *shen*, we also sink with her into this sense of emotional loss. Not only is she deep in the courtyard, and thus cut off from things outside the courtyard, but the layers of willow trees surrounding it give the sense of multiple screens or veils pulled down to further her isolation. By the end of line 3, then, we have a picture of a soul cut off from human contact.

The reason for her isolation is stated in line 4—her husband has disappeared on his richly ornamented horse and left her alone. Yet in this case, his destination is not to serve the Emperor; rather it is, euphemistically spoken, a "seductive journey" (l 4) on the "Zhangtai Road" (l 5). Each of these points to a destination that needs no further description.

She does the only thing left to her—mounting the steps to look in the direction of the Zhangtai Road in order to see him. But it is to no avail (l 5). This confirms the sense of her aloneness, and then we enter with her into her emotional isolation in lines 6-9. The driving rain and blustery wind (l 6) capture the unsettled nature of her heart. She would love to roll back the clock, and keep the late spring from disappearing, perhaps with the hope of restoring their relationship, but she is powerless to stop the passage of time.

Then, the poem closes with another image of her powerlessness. Her eyes turn from the Zhangtai Road to the courtyard to speak to her only companion: the flowers. She voices her complaint to them, but they don't speak (l 8). Rather, they fly away too (l 9). Everything that was supposed to bring stability and beauty in her life has vanished, gone with the chilly blast of the horse's departure, gone with the wind that carries away the flowers. Nothing and no one speaks to her, as she sinks deeper, deeper, deeper into her loneliness.

鹧鸪天·彩袖殷勤捧玉钟

晏几道 | 宋

彩袖殷勤捧玉钟[1]，
当年拚却醉颜红。
舞低杨柳楼心月，
歌尽桃花扇[2]底风。

从别后，忆相逢，
几回魂梦与君同。
今宵剩把银釭照[3]，
犹恐相逢是梦中。

zhè gū tiān cǎi xiù yīn qín pěng yù zhōng

yàn jǐ dào sòng

cǎi xiù yīn qín pěng yù zhōng
dāng nián pàn què zuì yán hóng
wǔ dī yáng liǔ lóu xīn yuè
gē jìn táo huā shàn dǐ fēng

cóng bié hòu yì xiāng féng
jǐ huí hún mèng yǔ jūn tóng
jīn xiāo shèng bǎ yín gāng zhào
yóu kǒng xiāng féng shì mèng zhōng

---

1 玉钟 – literally "jade bell," 钟 is used as a homophone for 盅, which is the character for a wine cup

2 桃花扇 – fan illustrated with peach blossoms; waved by a dancer in her performance

3 This line only describes the narrator raising his silver lamp, but it is implied he does this to see the person in front of him more closely

Partridge Sky·With Colorful Sleeves, you Eagerly Raised the Jade Cup
Yan Jidao | Song Dynasty

With colorful sleeves, you eagerly raised the jade cup;
In those days I didn't care if my face was flushed with drink.
You danced until the moon set in the willow branches;
You sang until you were too tired to wave your fan.

Since we parted, I've often thought of that meeting,
Many times, I dreamed of reuniting with you.
Tonight, I'm only concerned with lifting the silver lamp to see you,
My only fear is that this meeting, too, will be nothing but a dream.

The Poem in a Nutshell

In 56 well-chosen characters, Song Dynasty poet Yan Jidao captures the joy of a past celebration with his beloved, the pain of separation and the almost surrealistic experience of reunion. The story of that celebration is replete with sensual imagery: flowing and colorful sleeves, all-night dancing and drinking, and singing until exhaustion. Yet that time ended, with the joyous sounds fading to a distant memory. But now a reunion actually happens, a meeting whose shimmering prospects, but dangers, are captured in the glow of the silver lamp. Is it real or all just a dream?

Background

Though more than 230 of Yan Jidao's (1030?-1106?) poems survive in his 小山词, or "Small Mountain Poems," he is not nearly as well-known as his father Yan Shu (991-1055). The elder Yan was a poet, essayist, calligrapher and civil official, even rising to the position of chief advisor to the Emperor. Possessing a prodigious intellect, he passed the civil service examination at the unheard-of age of 14, composed more than 10,000 *ci* poems during his lifetime and was instrumental in establishing and strengthening a number of academic institutes in the Song Dynasty.

Yet after the father's death in 1055, his 20-something son Yan Jidao, as well as the more famous poet Ouyang Xiu, fell out of favor with the powers that be, and withdrew to practice his literary skill. Yan Jidao is one of the few who left us with a record about how his poems, and other *ci* poems, were collected at that time.

> "Those wild stanzas and drunken lines (i.e., the original poems) drifted about in the world along with singers and wine stewards.... From that time on they were transmitted with various degrees of remove, and textual errors accumulated. Then, on (Aug 7, 1089), the songs were assembled and placed in order by the Duke of Gaoping (Fan Chunren, 1027-1101)," quoted in Paul W Kroll, et al, *Reading Medieval Chinese Poetry,* p. 205.

The quotation tells us that many of the *ci* poems originated in the needs or demands of drinking parties, were sometimes delivered extemporaneously, and then passed through several hands before finally being collected by imperial or political initiative. Though the poem presented here no doubt rose out of the pain of lovers' separation, it too was probably sung in various venues to ease pain, heighten enjoyment and help people forget their current troubles.

Analysis

Yan Jidao's poem neatly divides into two stanzas, each of four lines. The first stanza speaks of the joys of remembered celebration, while the second describes the memories of that day as well as the worried feelings upon reunion of the lovers. Color and frenzied activity characterized the celebration; but the twice-appearing character 梦 ("dream") captures both the memories of that celebration as well as the realities of the poet as he writes.

First, the celebration. The initial characters are 彩袖 ("colorful sleeves"), drawing our attention not to the body that is moving (the arms), but to those flashing sleeves which eagerly raised the jade drinking cup. We can see the blur of color and the frenzied dancing; we can hear the music playing all night. But most of all, through the author's concise and vivid language, we can "see" the time pass because of the moon's movements. Literally we have, "The dance ended when the moon (fell) on the building's willow tree," giving us a memorable picture of the moonlight filtering through the trees and onto the building. The dance, literally, fell "low" (低) when the moon went from overhead to a "low" position. The music ended (尽) when the "wind" of peach blossom fan reached the "bottom" (底).

The celebration sparked memories, to be sure, but the poem heads quickly to the present. Now comes the reunion of the lovers, a meeting fraught with expectation and some fear. The meeting will take place at night, and the flickering (照) silver lamp (银缸) illumines the beloved when she appears. But because the lover has been living so long in dreams, his biggest fear is that this meeting, too, will be nothing more than a dream. His dream of love might simply fade into a shattered dream. Such is the fear of all separated lovers.

江城子·乙卯正月二十日夜记梦

苏轼 | 宋

jiāng chéng zǐ yǐ mǎo zhèng yuè èr shí rì yè jì mèng

sū shì song

[1]十年生死两茫茫，
不思量，
自难忘。
千里孤坟，
5 无处话凄凉[2]。
纵使相逢应不识，
尘满面[3]，鬓如霜。

夜来幽梦忽还乡，
小轩窗，
10 正梳妆。
相顾无言，
惟有泪千行[4]。
料得年年[5]肠断[6]处，
[7]明月夜，短松冈。

shí nián shēng sǐ liǎng máng máng
bù sī liang
zì nán wàng
qiān lǐ gū fén
wú chù huà qī liáng
zòng shǐ xiāng féng yīng bù shí
chén mǎn miàn bìn rú shuāng

yè lái yōu mèng hū huán xiāng
xiǎo xuān chuāng
zhèng shū zhuāng
xiāng gù wú yán
wéi yǒu lèi qiān háng
liào dé nián nián cháng duàn chù
míng yuè yè duǎn sōng gang

---

1 As common in traditional Chinese poetry, the subject of the sentence not indicated; we decided to translate with the subject "you," rather than "she," to reflect the intimate nature of the poem

2 凄凉 – miserable, desolate, bleak; suggesting the idea of a numbing solitude

3 尘满面 – literally "face full of dust;" suggests long preoccupation to other things and inattentiveness of one's appearance

4 泪千行 – literally "a thousand columns" of tears, suggesting an abundant flow of tears

5 年年 suggests annual memory of the date of her death

6 断肠 – literally "gut-breaking," a combination of gut-wrenching and heart-breaking; neither catches the literal aspect but we chose to render it as heartbreaking

7 This line does not mention the grave, but it is understood that "the place of heartbreak" is her grave

25 Classic Chinese Love Poems

Song of the Riverside City·A Dream on the Twentieth day of the First Month of the Year Yimao (1075)
Su Shi | Song Dynasty

Ten years, such a long time since you died,
I try not to think about you,
But you're impossible to forget.
A distance of a thousand miles from your solitary grave
Is no place to voice my loneliness.
Even if we met now, you wouldn't recognize me,
My face careworn, my hair white as frost.

Last night, a dream suddenly brought me back home,
At the window of our small room,
You were putting on your makeup.
We gazed at each other wordlessly,
Between us, a river of tears.
Year by year, I'll think of the same heartbreaking scene,
Your grave, a moonlit night, a hill of short pines.

The Poem in a Nutshell

This remarkable poem about his deceased wife by Song Dynasty poet Su Shi may neatly be divided into two equal stanzas. In the first seven lines he laments her loss but recognizes that he can only pay proper respects to her if he is standing by her grave, 1000 miles away. But social turmoil and his government responsibilities make that impossible. Perhaps driven by that reality, in the second seven lines, he has a dream of their earlier and happier days. He imagines a common domestic scene, but a scene drenched in tears because of his departure. Regret and longing fill the poem.

Background

Su Shi (1036-1101) was one of the most accomplished men of his or any generation of Chinese history. He not only excelled in composing several forms of contemporary poetry, but his essays, letters, calligraphy, painting and even gastronomic skill were renowned. At nineteen (in 1055), he married the love of his life, sixteen-year-old Wang Fu. But she died unexpectedly ten years later. In his grief he married her cousin, Wang Runzhi, partly no doubt to keep the memory of Wang Fu alive. His busy life as a civil servant took him to Shandong, a thousand miles from Sichuan, where he enjoyed life with Wang Fu and where she was buried. This poem, written a decade after her death, reflects on the sadness he felt at being unable to be close to her after her death.

Analysis

It only takes us three lines to realize we are in the presence of one of China's great poets. Su Shi's vivid description and ability to bring us immediately into the interior spaces of his mind is fully on display. The passage of a decade since he lost his wife had no doubt muted the sound of her voice and dulled the memory of her presence a bit, and Su Shi skillfully brings us into that loss in lines 2-3. "I try not to think about you, but you're impossible to forget." We think of him struggling with himself, trying to make his new life with Wang Runzhi work, but then the thoughts of Wang Fu flood his mind.

Lines 4-5 emphasize the stark reality that he now feels. His distance from her cannot be erased; he can't just go to a Shandong airport and be in Sichuan in two hours. The difference in culture, speech patterns, climate—almost everything between those two regions leads him to say that he can't really honor her properly while he is in Shandong and she is buried in her lonely grave in Sichuan.

And then, in lines 6-7, he mentions that even if they met, his haggard complexion and frost-white hair (at age 40!) would make him unrecognizable to her. We get the sense that some of the language is hyperbolic, as if he is trying to say that the pain of her death had profound and continuing effects on his body. That past is both very real to him and, at the same time, somewhat of a dream. He brings us both into the heartache and the dream.

Perhaps the "dreamy" nature of that memory of her actually stimulated him to write about his dream in lines 8-14, a dream that he just had of her. He was suddenly back in his hometown. She was healthy and well, applying her makeup (ll 8-10). We witness an alluring and surprisingly intimate scene of tranquil domestic bliss. She is putting on makeup, he is watching her—and perhaps she doesn't even know it.

But the harmony of this pleasant dreamy domestic scene is quickly shattered as they exchange glances. The glances are wordless but not meaningless, for the poet quickly adds that they shed copious rivers of tears (l 12). We are never told why the tears flow; two explanations are possible. Perhaps we are to understand that the tears mean they must separate from each other for him to pursue his civil service. Perhaps, also, the poem wants us to return to today, with her appearance in the dream confirming that she is, in fact, alive for him today, a reality that dissolves them both into tears.

After taking this long journey with the poet in imaginative space and time, he takes us finally (ll 13-14) to the scene of her grave, already mentioned in line 4. All he can do is constantly to return in his mind to this sad spectacle. But he doesn't end there. He doesn't just mention that it is a place of heartbreaking sadness (肠断处), but he gives us enough detail about this grave to evoke our heartfelt understanding and sympathy. The grave is bathed in bright moonlight and ringed by pine trees. Though it is his dream, we can almost see the place in *his* dream. We too, if we suffered such a loss, would also want to return there.

卜算子·我住长江头
李之仪 | 宋

我住长江[1]头，
君住长江尾。
日日思君不见君[2]，
共饮长江水。

此水几时休，
此恨[3]何时已。
只愿君心似我心，
定不负[4]相思意。

bǔ suàn zǐ wǒ zhù cháng jiāng tóu
lǐ zhī yí song

wǒ zhù cháng jiāng tóu
jūn zhù cháng jiāng wěi
rì rì sī jūn bù jiàn jūn
gòng yǐn cháng jiāng shuǐ

cǐ shuǐ jǐ shí xiū
cǐ hèn hé shí yǐ
zhī yuàn jūn xīn sì wǒ xīn
dìng bù fù xiāng sī yì

---

1 长江 – Yangtze River

2 The order of "long" and "not seeing" are reversed in the translation

3 恨 – has range of meanings from hatred to resentment to regret

4 负 – to betray

Prophet Song·I Live at the Source of the River
Li Zhiyi | Song Dynasty

I live at the source of the river,
You live at its end.
Though not seeing you, I daily long for you,
Together, we drink the same water.

Will these waters ever stop flowing?
Will my regret ever cease?
My fondest wish is that your heart is as mine,
For I certainly won't be untrue to this longing.

The Poem in a Nutshell

This memorable poem from the Song poet Li Zhiyi builds on the image of the ever-flowing Yangtze River to explore the emotions of separated lovers. The river serves both as a stimulus to consider how close the lovers really are, because they both drink from its water each day, and as a reminder of how permanent their separation seems to be. Yet the author will not let regret or disappointment have the last word. The longing kindled by absence and fed by the common source of drink, reflects a true love that won't be betrayed.

Analysis

Though more than 100 poems of Li Zhiyi are extant, this is by far his best-known. Li Zhiyi was a younger contemporary of Su Shi, a personality and creative spirit of immense importance at the end of the 11th century in the Northern Song Dynasty. Scholars have pointed to Su Shi's poetry from the Yuanyou period (1086-1094), when he was back in the capital and focusing on poetic form and topics of personal introspection, as being influential in shaping Li Zhiyi's work. Certainly 卜算子 reflects an earnest introspective spirit.

The poem's 45 characters take us from a declaration of one person's residence at the source of the Yangtze to that same person's most solemn affirmation of eternal love for the beloved. In the middle, we are treated to a mini-drama that draws us in by its transparent simplicity and heartfelt longing.

The first two sentences describe an apparently disappointing situation in hopeful terms. Lovers are separated from each other by the 3900 miles of the Yangtze River, the third longest river in the world. One of the pair is at its source, and the other at its end. Though the author's thoughts, longing, and nostalgia are real, the two lovers don't see each other. Yet, hope exists because of "gong" (共)—"together" they drink the waters of this river. Bodies divided, but hearts united.

Yet, the optimism of the first two sentences is called into question in the third. Repetition piles up and slows the action, much as the waters of the Yangtze sometimes seem not to be moving at all. Yet the waters keep flowing, interminably so. Rather than using this as an occasion to declare the "ever-flowing" nature of love, it triggers a feeling of regret. "Will my regret ever cease?" is the wrenching cry of one who knows that however much one can imagine the lover each day drinking water from the same river, this is a poor, poor substitute for the beloved's presence and scents and arms and legs.

But regret won't have the last word in this poem. The final sentence replaces the wrenching cry with an earnest wish. "I only wish" is the tone of the 只愿 that begins the last thought. "If I could have one wish that would be granted..." is the sense of it. That wish is that my friend's heart would be as mine. Even though the lovers are separated and the emotional temperature of the other is impossible to determine, the author knows her heart. She knows that the longing that consumes her heart is true, is reflective of their true feelings, is something that needs to be honored in the distance and celebrated in the daily act of drinking water.

All she can do, however, is to express her dedication to the truth of this longing. She won't betray it. May his heart beat with hers. May they, as it were, drink of a common cup as they quaff the river's water. Any who have felt the loneliness, fear, hope and even presence of the beloved when separated can understand this raw emotion, expressed so neatly in regulated form by Li Zhiyi.

鹊桥仙·纤云弄巧

què qiáo xiān xiān yún nòng qiǎo

秦观 | 宋

qín song song

纤云弄巧[1]，
飞星传恨，
银汉迢迢暗度。
金风玉露[2]一相逢，
5 便胜却人间无数。

xiān yún nòng qiǎo
fēi xīng chuán hèn
yín hàn tiáo tiáo àn dù
jīn fēng yù lù yī xiāng féng
biàn shèng què rén jiān wú shù

柔情似水，
佳期[3]如梦，
忍顾鹊桥归路。
两情若是久长时，
10 又岂在朝朝暮暮。

róu qíng sì shuǐ
jiā qī rú mèng
rěn gù què qiáo guī lù
liǎng qíng ruò shì jiǔ cháng shí
yòu qǐ zài zhāo zhāo mù mù

1 弄巧 – emphasis on the girl's skillful weaving of the clouds

2 金风玉露 – literally Golden Wind and Jade Dew; a traditional description of Autumn; appearing in famous Tang dynasty poet Li Shangyin's poem on the Double Seventh Festival

3 佳期 – a special time

Song of the God of the Magpie Bridge·Delicate Clouds Paint the Sky

Qin Guan | Song Dynasty

Delicate clouds paint the sky,
Shooting stars carry their regrets,
The lovers silently cross the vast Milky Way.
They meet in Autumn's golden wind—
A rendezvous that surpasses countless others on earth.

Feelings gentle as water,
Reunion as a dream,
How can they endure one last look at the magpie bridge?
When two hearts have such a long-lasting bond,
What's the need to be together every day?

The Poem in a Nutshell

One of the beauties of the deeply-revered and familiar story of the Cowherd and the Weaver Girl is that its message of lovers separated by an apparently insuperable barrier resonates with every generation. In this case, the lovers can only meet once a year, at the "Double Seventh" Festival (August). But rather than this being an excuse for sadness, the poet surprises us and asks, 'If love is so permanent, why does one need to be together all the time?' It is a stunning, but optimistic, reading of a potentially devastating reality.

Background

Many people have called the story of the Cowherd and Weaving Girl one of the four great or classic Chinese folk tales. It tells us that a mortal man (the Cowherd), thinking to tease seven bathing (goddess) sisters, took the clothes of one (the Weaving Girl). The other sisters dressed and returned heavenward, leaving their sister with the playful man. Eventually the two fell in love, married and had children. Bothered by the long absence of her daughter, the heavenly mother angrily recalled her daughter to heaven, giving her the task of weaving the clouds into colorful hues. Thinking further to separate the lovers, she placed her daughter at one side of the heavens (identified with the star Vega) and her lover/husband at the other (identified with the star Altair). Touched by the love of the Cowherd and Weaving Girl, the magpies gathered and decided to form a bridge on one day of the year, coinciding with the "Double Seventh" festival, where the long-separated lovers would unite by walking over the Magpie Bridge.

Analysis

Qin Guan's poem reflects on this tale from a unique angle. We can see its uniqueness by briefly mentioning an early poetic reflection on the tale from the Han Dynasty, nearly 1000 years before Qin Guan's time. In that collection of "Nineteen Old Poems," the tale is read as one of overwhelming sadness. The woman in love slaves away at the loom, staring dismayed at the surging river (the Milky Way) separating her from her lover, lost in lamentation. A meeting for one day in the year cannot overcome the overmastering sadness she feels.

Yet Qin Guan will read the myth in an unexpectedly positive way. The poem can be divided into three sections: Lines 1-5 present a movement that begins in sad aloneness but culminates in the joy of the couple's annual meeting. Lines 6-8 bring us down from the "high" of the meeting to a longing look at each other when the inevitability of separation happens. But then lines 9-10 reflect on the meaning of this love and the lovers' meeting, suggesting that for those whose love is strong, and even permanent, an infrequent meeting is enough. After all, if love is infinite, infinite love divided by 365 (i.e., one meeting a year) still will result in an infinite number of meetings.

The poem moves like a great wave, beginning (l 1) with the multi-hued clouds, the beautiful work of the Weaver Girl. Yet line 2 tells us that this work happens in the context of meteors (飞星), shooting in the skies and carrying as it were the lovers' messages of regret for not being able to meet. Then, in line 3, the tone changes. The lovers prepare to cross the Magpie Bridge to unite. Brilliantly placed in line 3 is 迢迢, "vast" or "expansive," to capture the great distance that the lovers must cross to be united. Yet, once they come together, that reunion is so explosive, so powerful, that it surpasses the innumerable common meetings of people on earth (l 5).

But they have to part, and lines 6-8 describe their reluctant parting. Lines 6-7 are each very short, perhaps capturing the vivid reality of their meeting with almost breathless utterances such as "like water" and "like a dream." Their separation is inevitable, and the longing glance back over the bridge of line 8 describes the pain of that separation.

Rather than leaving the lovers in their anguish, like many other poetic reflections, Qin Guan gives us a more positive reading of their relationship in lines 9-10. Their love is permanent. Even though they separate for almost the whole year, the permanence of that affection and attraction remains. Though Western cultures now have the phrase "24/7" to describe the constant presence that lovers want from each other, our author says basically that "one day a year" is enough. It is a most challenging perspective on a most intimate relationship.

一剪梅·红藕香残玉簟秋

yī jiǎn méi hóng ǒu xiāng cán yù diàn qiū

李清照 | 宋

lǐ qīng zhào sòng

红藕[1]香残玉簟[2]秋，

hóng ǒu xiāng cán yù diàn qiū

轻解罗裳，独上兰舟[3]。

qīng xiè luó cháng dú shǎng lán zhōu

云中[4]谁寄锦书[5]来？

yún zhōng shéi jì jǐn shū lái

雁字[6]回时[7]，月满西楼。

yàn zì huí shí yuè mǎn xī lóu

花自飘零水自流，

huā zì piāo líng shuǐ zì liú

一种相思，两处闲愁。

yī zhǒng xiāng sī liǎng chù xián chóu

此情无计可消除，

cǐ qíng wú jì kě xiāo chú

才下眉头[8]，却上心头。

cái xià méi tóu què shàng xīn tóu

---

1 红藕 – red lotus

2 玉簟 – literally "jade mat;" the jade here describes the smoothness and cool-ness of the bamboo

3 兰舟 – 兰 is a type of wood, usually interpreted to be magnolia; however the character 兰 is also often used to give an object a sense of refinement and elegance

4 云中 – literally "between the clouds;" translated as "beyond the clouds" to emphasize distance and the sense of longing

5 锦书 – writing that is embroidered on silk scrolls; also describes letters that are cherished by the receiver

6 雁字 – literally "a character of geese;" describes v-shaped formation geese use when migrating

7 回时 – time of return; interpreted to be spring since that's when geese return to the north

8 眉头 – literally "brows;" translated to show contrast between what the brain thinks and what the heart feels

A Cut Plum Blossom: The Lotus has Withered, yet its Scent Lingers; I Lie Upon my Autumn-chilled Bamboo Mat

Li Qingzhao | Song Dynasty

The lotus has withered yet its scent lingers; I lie upon my autumn-chilled bamboo mat,
Gently I untie my silk skirt and alone board the exquisite boat.
Who will send me winged messages from beyond the clouds?
It will be the wild geese when they return in the spring, when the moonlight spills over the West tower.

But the flowers just float along, and the water returns to its course,
One type of lovesick longing, two places of quiet grief.
There is no remedy for this heartache,
It descends from my head, only to coil around my heart.

The Poem in a Nutshell

This poem discloses the conflicting thoughts and feelings of a wife who longs to be reunited with her traveling husband. On the one hand, her "thinking self" gives her hope. He is away, but she can board her exquisite boat, launch into the river, look heavenward and imagine a sweet message coming from him, perhaps even brought courtesy of the geese soaring overhead. On the other hand, her "feeling self" realizes that there really is no way to bridge the distance. Nature's flowers fade; the water gently returns to its place. Rather than a feeling of connection or unity, all that is left is "One type of lovesick longing, two places of quiet grief." There is no way to dispel her numbing sadness.

Background

Li Qingzhao (1084-1151) is one of the best-known female poets in Chinese history. Raised in a family of government officials and scholars in the capital city of Shandong Province, she quickly developed a deep knowledge of Chinese poetry and history. At 18 she married a distinguished young man Zhao Mingcheng, whose father was later appointed prime minister of the Song dynasty. She and her husband shared a mutual love for poetry, literature and ancient Chinese culture. Yet, her husband also studied at the Imperial Academy hundreds of miles away, and this led to frequent and long separations. After only two years of marriage, while her husband was away, Li Qingzhao penned this poem of loneliness and longing.

The eight lines of the poem are written according to the poetic convention known as the *ci*. Originating several hundred years earlier, *ci* poetry was distinguished from its predecessors in that every line had to meet a tonal and rhythmic convention. That convention is captured in the title of the poem—that is, the title doesn't tell the reader anything about the contents but rather tells us the melody and rhythm of the poem. There were around 800 *ci* patterns, making the mastery of this genre of poetry the task of a lifetime. We don't know the melodies suggested by the title; all that we have is a deep outpouring of grief at the separation of young lovers.

Analysis

This 60-character poem neatly divides into two parts of four lines each. Though loneliness is the overwhelming sensation of the entire poem, the first half focuses less on separation than on the hope of receiving a future message from her husband. But in the second half of the poem, reality has set in. There will be no incoming letter. The only shared reality is distance. Though they might have a common longing, a common lovesickness, each must bear his or her private grief in the solitude of their individual places.

Lines 1-4 stimulate our sensual palette by appealing to the senses of smell, touch and sight. We *smell* the lingering odor of the withered lotus; we *feel* the damp and chilled smooth bamboo mat on which she reclines; we *see* her rising, laying aside her garments and clambering alone onto the boat (ll 1-2). Four words in the first two lines enhance the sense references: we have a "red" (红) lotus, a jade-smooth (玉) mat, a silk (罗) skirt and a magnolia (兰) boat. Though she sleeps alone, she will be further alone with her thoughts by casting off in the boat. The broad expanse of sky above and the luminous clouds invite her to focus on the air, rather than the land or boat. Can there be a messenger, a courier beyond the clouds, who will bring a letter from her beloved? (l 3). Lines 3-4 are closely connected in thought because of the ancient belief that geese, which flew from north to south and back again, were couriers, bringing letters to separated lovers. Thus, her mention of the geese is not accidental. She gazes heavenward and is encouraged. Perhaps a flying messenger will bring her good tidings of her love.

But then, in the second half of the poem (ll 5-8) reality sets in. Once her eyes return from the heavens to the water, the truth of her longing dawns fully on her. The flowers wither and float aimlessly in the water. Then she seemingly turns and looks behind the boat, only to see the waters return to their normal course and flow. Hope may rise in the breast, but nothing really changes. The deafening silence of the water that flows by itself, that flows in its natural way (自留), tells her that her aloneness is real, and lasting. Realization of this brings her to her final thought (ll 7-8). The hearts of young lovers share a common bond, but they are separated by an unbridgeable gulf. All that is left is "this feeling" (此情), this heartache that cannot be dispelled, this sickness of heart that can't be cured. It leaves the brain and then coils tight around the heart (l 8). The movement of the last line is significant. We have movement "down" (下) from the head and "up" (上) to the heart. But it is of no avail. Unfulfilled lovesick yearning is the last sentiment.

青玉案·元夕　　　　　　　　　　**qīng yù àn yuán xī**
辛弃疾 | 宋　　　　　　　　　　*xīn qì jí song*

东风夜放¹花千树²，　　　　　　dōng fēng yè fàng huā qiān shù
更³吹落，星如雨。　　　　　　　gèng chuī luò xīng rú yǔ
宝马雕车香满路。　　　　　　　bǎo mǎ diāo chē xiāng mǎn lù
凤箫⁴声动，　　　　　　　　　　fèng xiāo shēng dòng
5　玉壶⁵光转，　　　　　　　　　yù hú guāng zhuǎn
一夜鱼龙舞。　　　　　　　　　　yī yè yú lóng wǔ

蛾儿雪柳⁶黄金缕，　　　　　　　é ér xuě liǔ huáng jīn lǚ
笑语盈盈暗香去。　　　　　　　xiào yǔ yíng yíng àn xiāng qù
众里寻他⁷千百度，　　　　　　　zhòng lǐ xún tā qiān bǎi dù
10　蓦然回首，　　　　　　　　　mò rán huí shǒu
那人却在，　　　　　　　　　　nà rén què zài
灯火阑珊处。　　　　　　　　　　dēng huǒ lán shān chù

1　放 – suggests setting off fireworks, as used in the context of 放烟花

2　树 – functions as a measure word here to show the number of blooms

3　更 – "furthermore; even more so," suggests the windblown fireworks is even more impressive than the blaze of the thousand blossoms

4　凤萧 – 凤 means phoenix; in this case, it refers to an ornate flute

5　玉壶 – literally a jade pot; symbolizes the full moon

6　蛾儿雪柳 – refers to two types of hair ornaments, translated to include only the latter

7　The character 他 is in the middle of the line, making *him* the focus of the search

Song of the Green Jade Plate·Lantern Festival
Xin Qiji/ Song Dynasty

The east wind sets ablaze a thousand blossoms in the night,
Blowing down the fireworks in a rain of stars.
Richly decorated carriages drawn by horses pave the streets with their scent,
The melodious flute echoes,
The moon sheds its light,
The night puts on a dance of fish and dragons.

Girls adorned with silver willows and golden tulle dresses,
They leave a trail of gentle laughter and subtle fragrance.
I search everywhere in the throng for him,
I suddenly turn my head,
And there he is,
In the dim lights.

The Poem in a Nutshell

With its shimmering lanterns, cascading fireworks, melodious music and thronging crowds, the Lantern Festival described in this poem captures our hearts. We see a twofold movement in the poem. First is an exterior one, where the narrator moves from the noisy crowd to a silent space. Then, there is an interior one, as the fireworks streaking the sky become the fireworks blazing in the heart. Whether by arrangement or happenstance, the narrator turns her eyes in the silent dimness of the night and sees the object of her desire standing right there. There he is! Sometimes your life, and love, is where you least expect it.

Background

This poem, with its well-known last two lines, is the creation of the Song military leader and poet Xin Qiji (1140-1207). Born in Shandong when the north was being overrun by the Jurchens, a nomadic people from further north and east, Xin Qiji was taught to despise the invaders. Due to later military achievements, he attained a high post at the Song Court in the south, but his more aggressive policy of retaliation against the Jurchens became out of step with the dominant tone at court. Thus, at the height of his powers, he was sidelined, and he moved to Jiangxi to take up poetry. More than 600 of his poems survive; he has often been compared favorably even to Su Shi, the dean of Song *ci* poetry.

Analysis

With imaginative brilliance and powerful descriptions, our poet depicts the festive environment of the Lantern Festival, held on the 15th day of the First Lunar Month (early February). The first half of the poem depicts the scene in all its sensuous richness. We *feel* the cool east wind, an auspicious wind, as it rustles the trees and wafts 1000s of glistening fireworks in the sky. The opening line has a certain ambiguity: either the wind is blowing lanterns that bedeck 1000 trees or the wind is, as it were, fanning the fireworks exploding overhead. We then *see* the exploding fireworks as they rain down like falling stars on the awed observers.

Not content with these two senses, the author lets us *smell* the richly caparisoned horses drawing the scented carriages as they move down the road, shedding odor like incense as if in a parade or festive procession. Coupled with that is the haunting *sound* of the flute playing as the moon shines high in the sky. All night long there are the sinuous movements of dancers, dressed up in costumes of fish and dragons or, possibly, lanterns that so dance. We can almost *touch* it all.

But then, in the second half, the scene shifts to the people at the festival. A crowd of girls is decked out for the occasion, with silver willow and butterfly-shaped hairpieces and golden-flecked dresses.

They laugh lightly, giggling at stories that girls tell each other, with the scent of perfume wafting along in their wake.

One of them breaks away from the group, seeking something different than what the crowd of girls can supply. As the poem tells us, she "seeks him in 100,000 places." Light giggling turns into earnest search in those few words. We see that the festival is also the occasion not just for fireworks and riddles on lanterns, but for love. Does she know the one she seeks, or is she just driven by the longings of the heart, a heart that will search everywhere until she finds him? We are never told.

She retreats to the quiet and dark spaces, a stark contrast to the light and boisterous activity of the first part. She searches earnestly, but to no avail. But then, in the most dramatic thirteen characters of this or hundreds of poems, we have "Suddenly, she turns her head and there he is! There he is, where the lights are dim."

The poem need say no more. Our imaginations take over. But the poem has perfectly led us to this place, taking us from light to dimness, from a crowd to an individual, from fireworks raining from above to fireworks welling up in the heart. We leave with a sense of immense hopefulness, that maybe in our own lives we will find meaning, and perhaps even the love of our lives, away from the bustle of the crowd, where the light has come to an end.

摸鱼儿 · 雁邱词
元好问 | 宋

mō yú ér yàn qiū cí
yuán hào wèn song

问世间，	wèn shì jiān
情为何物，	qíng wéi hé wù
直教生死相许。	zhí jiào shēng sǐ xiāng xǔ
天南地北双飞客，	tiān nán dì běi shuāng fēi kè
5 老翅几回寒暑。	lǎo chì jǐ huí hán shǔ
欢乐趣，离别¹苦，	huān lè qù lí bié kǔ
就中更有痴儿女。	jiù zhōng gèng yǒu chī ér nǔ
君应有语，	jūn yīng yǒu yǔ
渺万里层云，	miǎo wàn lǐ céng yún
10 千山暮²雪，	qiān shān mù xuě
只影向谁去。	zhī yǐng xiàng shuí qù
横汾路，	héng fén lù
寂寞当年萧鼓³，	jì mò dāng nián xiāo gǔ
荒烟依旧平楚。	huāng yān yī jiù píng chǔ
15 招魂楚些何嗟及⁴，	zhāo hún chǔ suò hé jiē jí
山鬼暗啼风雨。	shān guǐ àn tí fēng yǔ
天也妒，	tiān yě dù
未信与，	wèi xìn yǔ
莺儿燕子俱黄土。	yīng ér yàn zǐ jù huáng tǔ
20 千秋万古，为留待骚人， ⁵	qiān qiū wàn gǔ wèi liú dài sāo rén
狂歌痛饮，	kuáng gē tòng yǐn
来访雁邱处。	lái fǎng yàn qiū chù

---

1 离别 – departure; in this case the departure is the death of one goose

2 暮 – dusk; adds to the melancholic atmosphere

3 Contemporary sources recount Emperor Wu of Han, accompanied with the pomp of his office, used to travel through the area

4 嗟 – to sigh; our translation captures the emotion of this line

5 Though not stated explicitly in the line, the geese's love is implied here and is reflected in the translation

Song of the Fish·Poem of the Geese's Tomb
Yuan Haowen | Song Dynasty

Of all the things in the world, I ask,
What kind of thing is love
That it binds creatures together in life and death?
From pole to pole they soared inseparable,
Old wings carrying them through frigid winters and torrid summers.
What utter pleasures! But parting brought such bitterness,
More than humans are they madly in love.
He must have seen
That there would be a bleak, endless, cloud-filled journey,
Over thousands of snow-clad mountains.
To whom would his lone shadow go?

Along the Fen River,
Lonely after the resounding music faded,
Desolation reclaims the barren plain.
I beckon their spirits to no avail,
The mountain goddess weeps in the wind and the rain,
Heaven is envious,
That they will not,
As larks and swallows, turn to dust.
Instead, for all time, their love invites poets
To nurse wild songs in their hearts, and drink as
They visit the geese's tomb.

The Poem in a Nutshell

This Song Dynasty poem uses an unforgettable story about the commitment of a pair of geese to each other to muse on the nature of love and to memorialize the fidelity of the geese, a fidelity which exceeds that of humans to each other.

Background

Yuan Haowen (1190-1257) lived during one of the most unstable and violent times in Chinese history. The Jin in the North and the Song in the South wearied themselves out against each other in a century of fighting as the Yuan (Mongols) patiently stood by, waiting for their opportunity to divide the spoils and take over. They finally did so about two decades after Yuan Haowen's death. Because of this turbulence, many of his poems focus on the brutality of war and the vulnerability of the common people. A new style of poetry associated with his name, called the 丧乱, captures the bloodshed and tragic disaster of that time.

Yet this poem is about love, and behind it lies the experience of the poet at about 15 years of age. While traveling near home he happened upon a hunter, with two dead geese, who told him the story of capturing the geese. Both flew into his net, but one escaped. Seeing his companion trapped, and soon to be killed, the escaped goose didn't fly away but rather plummeted to the earth, killing himself. So touched was the poet by this story that he bought the geese and buried them by the Fen River, erecting a small monument to commemorate this "more than human" love of geese for each other. This poem reflects on that love and the imagined decision-making of the living one of the pair just before plunging to his death.

Analysis

We have divided the poem into 22 short lines. Often the meaning of a line is crystal clear, but on several occasions the author uses ambiguous or partial images that can lead to significantly different readings of this poem. This analysis tries to make sense of the whole and highlight a few difficult areas of interpretation.

Lines 1-8 pose a question about the nature of love and then rhapsodize imaginatively on the faithful love of two geese for each other. The question posed is time-honored but no less urgent for being so. It is, 'What is this thing we call love that couples go through so much, through life and death really, to connect deeply to each other?' It is a fine question, one that makes our hearts soar just as the geese soar in the next few lines.

Rather than providing an abstract answer, the poet imagines the love of these now-dead geese for each other. They must have soared inseparably, braving torrid summers and frigid winters to be with each other. Their love even exceeded (更) that of humans for each other.

Lines 9-11 briefly reflect on what it must have been like for the surviving bird, the one escaping the net, in those brief moments between escape and his own death. He realized that life alone wasn't worth living. His emotional bleakness is well-captured by the poet's images of vast empty spaces of cloud-covered terrain.

Lines 12-14 take us to the spot of burial, by the Fen River. This place was the regular spot of the imperial patrol and frolic, filled with the loud and celebratory din of music. But that din has died out, and all that remains on that spot is a lone monument, testifying to the love of the geese for each other.

The poet is saddened, and in lines 15-19, he beckons the spirits of the dead geese (though some interpret this as the spirit of the deceased emperor) but to no avail. Even the mountain goddess of the region is of no use. But then, an idea crosses the poet's mind. Perhaps heaven after all is jealous of these geese because they will live on in poetic memory, while the millions of larks and swallows just turn to dust.

Then, in the concluding lines 20-22, the author speaks of the reason why the geese will never be forgotten. His poem will attract poets to the memorial cairn, and they will drink and celebrate while they too muse on the wondrous love of these geese.

清

QING DYNASTY

1644-1911 CE

浣溪沙 · 谁念西风独自凉

huàn xī shā shéi niàn xī fēng dú zì liáng

纳兰性德 | 清

nà lán xìng dé qīng

谁念西风[1]独自凉，
萧萧黄叶闭疏窗[2]，
沉思往事[3]立残阳。

shéi niàn xī fēng dú zì liáng

xiāo xiāo huáng yè bì shū chuāng

chén sī wǎng shì lì cán yáng

被酒莫惊春[4]睡重，[5]
赌书[6]消得泼茶香，
当时只道是寻常。

bèi jiǔ mò jīng chūn shuì zhòng

dǔ shū xiāo dé pō chá xiāng

dāng shí zhǐ dào shì xún cháng

---

1 西风 – the western wind is a symbol of bleakness

2 疏窗 – windows that have intricately carved wooden frames, here rendered "patterned"

3 往事 – things of the past

4 春 – spring, which contrasts the current autumn setting

5 被酒莫惊春睡重 – lacks a subject and is unclear whether it refers to the poet or his wife; the translation honors this vagueness

6 赌书 – a game where the players guess lines in particular scrolls and books; an intellectual challenge

25 Classic Chinese Love Poems

Song of the Creek Washers·Who Cares that I am so Alone in the Cold Autumn Wind

Nalan Xingde | Qing Dynasty

Who cares that I am so alone in the cold autumn wind,
The yellow leaves rustle, I close my patterned windows,
Deep in thought, I stand in the waning sunlight.

Don't startle the dreamer, drunk with heavy spring sleep,
We gambled, whiling away the time amid the scent of spilled tea,
Back then, I took everything for granted.

The Poem in a Nutshell

This magnificent poem from the early Qing Dynasty scholar and public official Nalan Xingde contrasts the empty feeling of current loss with the buoyant experience of joyful normalcy that once characterized his life. His young wife had died in childbirth, leaving him alone with his memories of carefree springtime pleasure, intellectual games and, most subtly, the enduring aroma of spilled tea. What lends the poem its peculiar power is the assumption that the free-flowing connection he enjoyed with his wife was what should characterize "normal" life. Isn't it "normal" to have such a pleasant life? Yet, with half of the poem devoted to the windswept chill of the present, the author and reader feel deeply the evanescent character of what we often take for granted, for normal.

Background

Nalan Xingde (1655-1685), whose loss of his wife captivates us in the poem, was himself short-lived, dying in his 31st year. He was descended from Manchu nobility and was related to the Emperor through his father. His education was first-rate, and his life had all the indicia of a rising star—successful passage of exams, prominent government posts, publication of a book of poetry by his mid-20s. Indeed, one of his enduring scholarly contributions was his edition of hundreds of commentaries on the Confucian Classics, an edition that to this day includes some commentators who are otherwise unknown. Yet his life was scarred by death of his wife in childbirth while both were in their early twenties. This poem describes the lingering feelings attending that loss.

Analysis

This six-line, forty-two-character poem consists of two neatly-balanced stanzas, one describing the past and the other describing the present. Yet, rather than presenting the two in their historical order, the author moves from present to the past. Characterizing the present is a bleak cold wind, blowing fall leaves and an overpowering sense of aloneness. Characteristic of the past was joyful spring drunkenness, playful games with his wife and the sweet savor of spilled tea. The sensual richness of each period speaks clearly to us. The most enduring feeling the poem leaves us is the sense that life's most precious things are often taken for granted, taken for normal and that they can, without ceremony, be swiftly taken from us.

His present experience (ll 1-3) consists of two movements: the movement of chilled bleakness and the movement of turning within to dredge up a painful memory. The movement of chilled bleakness opens with a plaintive question. "Who really cares?" is the tone of it. Who really cares if the cold west wind rips through me? Who really cares if I am dreadfully alone in this cold, cold wind? The rustling leaves and cold wind send a chill through him; by closing the window he not only protects himself against the wind and leaves, but he also draws further into himself. Once the window is secured, the fruit of that inward journey is evident: he thinks deeply on the past as he faces the waning sunlight. The sun's fire is dying; the leaves have no more life; all that is left is a swirling mass of leaves in the cold fall air. And his thoughts.

His thoughts (ll 4-6) take him to a happier time when the singular aloneness of the present was replaced by the sounds of lovers playing and celebrating. Spring revelries led to sleeping pleasures; afterwards, they engaged in intellectual competition. Described here only as, literally, "gambling with books," the game or competition probably consisted of one person mentioning a line of poetry and possibly placing a bet on where it was located in a stack of books and scrolls they had with them. Precise identification of poetic lines or philosophical fragments has always been a Chinese intellectual challenge; the highly-educated and can-do-it-all young-twenties couple eagerly played the game, spilling tea in the process, with the abiding aroma of that tea permeating not only the room but the memory of that most pleasant time.

The last line serves to bring the poet back to reality—to the present that he doesn't enjoy. When they were in their "salad days," to quote Shakespeare, they felt as if it their situation was one of joyful normalcy. What could intervene to take away the sense of aesthetic and physical pleasure that was at their fingertips? It was so normal to eat and drink in the warm spring days. It was so normal to drink tea and challenge each other intellectually. It was a good life, but such a normal-seeming one. At least, that's how it all felt at that time.

But normalcy faded quickly when tragedy intervened. All that are left are the swirling leaves and faded memories. There is no shaking of fists against fortune or a divine figure, as in the Book of Job, no thundering complaints of "Why me?" or eloquent appeals to a higher sense of justice in the world. The most that can be said is that a wistful longing and quiet sadness covers the author, just as the rustling leaves cover his patterned window.

绮怀诗十六首其十五
黄景仁 | 清

qǐ huái shī shí liù shǒu qí shí wǔ
huáng jǐng rén qīng

几回花下[1]坐吹箫，
银汉红墙[2]入望遥。
似此星辰非昨夜，
为谁风露立中宵。

jǐ huí huā xià zuò chuī xiāo
yín hàn hóng qiáng rù wàng yáo
sì cǐ xīng chén fēi zuó yè
wèi shuí fēng lù lì zhōng xiāo

缠绵思尽[3]抽残[4]茧，
宛转心伤剥后蕉[5]。
三五年时三五月[6]，
可怜杯酒不曾消。

chán mián sī jìn chōu cán jiǎn
wǎn zhuǎn xīn shāng bāo hòu jiāo
sān wǔ nián shí sān wǔ yuè
kě lián bēi jiǔ bù céng xiāo

---

1 花下 – literally "under the flowers"

2 银汉红墙 – quoting Tang era poet Li Shangying who uses this image to
   describe a red wall separating two people. We also previously discussed Qin
   Han's poem on the magpie bridge, where the 银汉 is the Milky Way that sepa-
   rates the lovers

3 缠绵思尽 – "思" is a homophone of "丝," used here as a wordplay to compare
   the "threads of longing" to the cocoon spun by silkworms; adding to the silk
   imagery are the first two characters, which both have the silk radical

4 残 carries the meaning of something that is injured, disabled, or incomplete;
   implies that the worm cannot live in an unfinished cocoon

5 剥后蕉 – literally a peeled banana; rendered as "discarded banana peel" to
   emphasize the vulnerability and uselessness the narrator feels

6 三五月 – the fifteenth of the lunar month, a full moon; captured in our transla-
   tion with the phrase "bathed in the moonlight"

25 Classic Chinese Love Poems

Fifteenth of Sixteen Poems of Beautiful Reveries
Huang Jingren | Qing Dynasty

How often I played the flute in the garden,
The red wall separating us as I gaze into the distance.
But the stars are not those of former nights,
For whom do I stand in the midnight wind and dew?

My lingering feelings are drawn out like silk, leaving me in an incomplete cocoon,
My tender heart is injured like a discarded banana peel.
Bathed we were in the moonlight of your fifteenth year,
It's a pity I can't drown the memory in wine.

The Poem in a Nutshell

Poems of separation are numerous and almost always terribly sad, but few reach the depths of loneliness as this 56-character poem by Qing Dynasty poet Huang Jingren. Though the poem's language is often metaphorical and allusive, we can't mistake the sense that separation means the end of the poet's life— an "incomplete cocoon" is by definition a cocoon that doesn't allow the silkworm to morph into an adult moth. Incomplete and discarded, the poet feels overwhelmed by loss.

Background

Huang Jingren (1749-1783) lived much closer to our times than he did to his literary idol, the late-Tang poet Li Shangyin. Li's poetry, immortalized in the previously discussed 琴瑟, also used vivid yet elusive imagery to capture the fleeting character of love. Though closer in time to us than to the Tang Dynasty, Huang Jingren's words and phrases owe more to the ancient than to a more modern period.

He lived only to age 34, but in those years he composed many poems, 1300 of which still survive. He lived during the heyday and prosperity of the Qing Dynasty, presided over by the 61 year-long rule of the Qianlong Emperor (1735-96). Yet, the stability of that rule wasn't reflected in his life. Orphaned at age 4, but with talents widely recognized, he wandered through Zhejiang, Anhui, Jiangsu and Hebei provinces. He didn't do well in the imperial examinations and had no regular employment. Some of his poems reflect the hardship of his poverty and the loneliness of being of scholarly temperament in an unappreciative society. On one occasion he wrote that he felt like an insect in autumn that merely emits its chirps. Yet, he also knew love and wrote about the pain of separation from his beloved in a 16-part masterpiece, of which our poem is "Poem 15."

Analysis

Unlike other poets, who firmly anchored their poetry in a certain period of the year (the Lantern Festival) or a well-known story (the Cowherd and Weaver Girl), this poem emerges solely from the poet's memory. It is linked with no particular place or time. But Huang's unspoken point is that the interior spaces of the heart need no geography or calendar to be well-explored.

The poem consists of eight lines, each of seven characters. The last character of the first and final lines is xiāo. Several other lines end with the rhyming yáo or xiāo or jiāo. Just as the memory of his departed love leaves him feeling incomplete, so that "incompleteness" is reflected in the final rhyming patterns: 5 of the 8 lines end in "ao."

Past and present run together, as there are few indications as to which line refers to the present and which line to the past. One of the clear references to time is line 1, where he recalls playing the doleful lute on numerous occasions. But then things become hazy. Drawing upon the nebulous imagery of Li Shangyin, he mentions that a red wall, probably in the courtyard where he was playing, was like the "Milky Way" that separated them as he gazed into the distance (l 2). Perhaps they were already separated and the "wall as Milky Way" solidifies the distance. Mention of heavenly stars leads to his mention in line 3 of the stars of the present not being like those of the past. He is standing under them, alone, drenched with the midnight dew (l 4), a broken man.

Often the second group of four lines of such a poem would have a more upbeat tone. We could even compose it in our mind. "Even though we are separated, I still feel you..." or something like that. But Huang won't let us get away with platitudes. The imagery now turns to death and uselessness. What good is a partial or incomplete cocoon (l 5)? The silkworm who hasn't finished his job cannot emerge to the life of a moth. Our poet feels like that. Of what use is the bruised covering of a banana? Once it is peeled, it is not useful for anything. Though we might chuckle at the seeming incongruity of a heart's being damaged like a banana peel, the two images from nature powerfully point to the strong feeling that his life was over. With his actual death at age 34, he may not have been too wide of the mark.

The poem concludes with the poet returning in memory to the earlier day, one of those many days when he played the lute in the garden. She was in her prime (15 years old), and the moon was full. The scene was pregnant with such awesome possibilities. But it didn't work out. All he can think of is burying himself in the oblivion of drink. He would not have been the first to have reacted that way to the pain of lost love.

AUTHOR BIOGRAPHIES

 **EURYDICE CHEN** is a recent graduate of Willamette University with a B.A. in Economics. Since moving to the States in 2006, she has continued her study of the Chinese language and culture on her own and has been involved in many Chinese-English translation projects. She has had a long-time interest in Chinese poetry and offers a unique cultural perspective on traditional references in the contemporary context. Eurydice was part of the student translation team for Dr. Juwen Zhang's book, *Metafolklore: Stories of Sino-US Folkloristic Communication* (*Volume One*), published in 2017.

 **WILLIAM R LONG**, M Div, Ph D, J D, is an award-winning author who has written more than 20 books in biblical studies, biography, legal history, education theory, the study of words, and classical civilizations. He has been a professor of religion and humanities, history and government, and law, as well as a pastor, editorial writer and litigation attorney. He currently is completing a commentary on Confucius' Analects.

CPSIA information can be obtained
at www.ICGtesting.com
Printed in the USA
LVHW090550291220
675308LV00006B/134